Inheritance
&Succession
The Complete Irish Guide

John G. Murphy & Jason Dunne

Introduction

Every day thousands of families in Ireland comprising fathers, mothers, sons, daughters, in-laws, nieces, nephews, uncles, aunts, grandparents, great-grandchildren and cousins are either worried about or affected by the issues of inheritance and succession.

Many Irish living abroad are similarly affected whether it's about care for a loved one, their own possibility of inheriting a fortune or concern that the 'wrong' person will get the home place.

Statements based on statistical and anecdotal information tell us that in Ireland in 2008:

- Many family members may be at war over wills, inheritance and succession matters.

- Half of adults over the age of 18 may not have made a will.

- Only two out of ten business people may have identified who their successor might be and two out of every three family businesses will fail in the next generation.

Most lawyers find an increase in the number of court cases over land, inheritances, divorces and separations. The cost in some cases is that assets have to be sold and proceeds divided, with a large portion of those proceeds going to the lawyers.

In our experience, most of the challenges that are being experienced or that lie ahead for families throughout Ireland can be eased or avoided altogether. As solicitors, we have witnessed the joy of many and the disappointment, lost opportunities, unrealistic expectations and pain and suffering of others.

We believe that for 95% of problems there is a solution, and that families need not end up in a waste of time and energy, courtroom battles for years to come or legacies to generations of sadness or hatred.

Inheritance and Succession – The Complete Irish Guide is the first book of its kind in Ireland to offer people a life long approach to their inheritance and succession situations.

The latest statistics from the Central Statistics Office show that:
• More than one million people in Ireland are over the age of 50.
• The number of divorced people has risen by 70% between 2002 and 2006.
• Cohabiting couples, most with children, accounted for 11.6% of all family units in 2006.
• Lone parents, (mothers and fathers), accounted for 17% of all family units in 2006.

Our rapidly changing demographic, social and economic conditions present new challenges in managing, creating and transferring wealth, planning gradual succession, giving and gaining from inheritance, and in providing for all parties as fairly and as sensitively as possible.

This book brings together information to tackle complex legal, tax and financial matters in this area and it assists young and old in making their life, succession, inheritance and investment plans.

It will help single people and those who are married, co-habiting, separated or divorced. It also gives guidance towards care of children and dependants.

Knowledge is power and we hope that by reading this book you will be empowered. We advise that you use this information as an aid to consultation and advice with qualified, registered professional advisers.

Our objective is to clarify the issues, help people to avoid mistakes, and present a way through which to achieve a positive result. We will be delighted if in the process we help people towards outcomes of happiness.

You can change lives. The best place to start is with your own life. The best time to begin is now.

Leave this place in a better condition than that in which you found it. - Anon

Acknowledgments

Many people contributed in different ways towards the production of this book. These included our family members, fellow lawyers, researchers, secretaries, writers, journalists, photographers, designers and printers.

Our special thanks to Trish Malone, associate editor, Jim Buckley of www.soundadvice.ie, consultant editor, John Boyle for opinion, Liam Mulcahy, Ibar Carty, Ger Carty, Mick Quinn for photography, Simon Daniels of Design for Life for visual concepts, layout and design, Gerry Curran, Courts Service for images, istockphoto.com for stock photography, Ciaran Muldowney, Cactus, for use of Russian Dolls.

Sean O'Keeffe and Peter O'Connell of Liberties Press for their encouragement, Michael Doyle, South East Radio for play excerpt, Declan Lyons of BCT Communications Ltd for opinion, Paul Browne of Browne's Funeral Directors for information, Central Statistics Office for statistical information, Health Service Executive (HSE) for information.

Mr. Justice Robert Barr for encouragement and endorsement.

Staff of John A. Sinnott & Co. Solicitors for their dedicated assistance and background research, Michael O'Leary of Michael O'Leary & Co. auditors and accountants for opinion, Nicholas Furlong for historical insight, and Louise Murphy, Siobhan Dunne and Brigid Freeman for their support.

The inspiration to produce this book comes from the experiences of the many families for whom we have provided service.

We thank them all.

Disclaimer
Every effort has been made to ensure that the information provided in this book is both accurate and up to date. If you notice any errors or omissions, we would appreciate if you would let us know as soon as possible.

The information provided is of a general nature.

The publishers and authors and their servants or agents assume no responsibility for and give no guarantees, undertakings or warranties concerning the accuracy, completeness or up-to-date nature of the information provided in this publication at this time and do not accept any liability whatsoever arising from any errors or omissions.

If you need advice, consult with a trusted qualified adviser.

Cover photography: Mick Quinn Photography. www.mqphoto.com

Cover Image: Russian Maryoshka dolls, traditional symbols of family love and happiness.

The Authors

John G. Murphy and Jason Dunne have many years of experience and expertise in urban and rural areas dealing with inheritance, succession and related matters.

John G. Murphy

In 28 years as a solicitor, John G. Murphy has handled cases in commercial matters, farm and residential, probate/tax, litigation (commercial, personal injury, property), and employment law. His extensive client base includes private, business, corporate and State sectors. He deals with family, arbitration, insurance, labour and criminal law. He is also an adviser to voluntary workshops, charities, and major corporates involved in the supermarket, property and bio-fuel business. He is a member of the criminal legal aid panel, the family civil legal aid panel, and the legal panel for Mental Health tribunals.

Jason Dunne

Jason Dunne qualified as a solicitor in 2007. He has more than 20 years of experience in the legal profession. He deals with wills, probate, related litigation, and tax issues for clients in Ireland and abroad.

Foreword

In the modern era Irish law has been, by and large, well served by text book writers. However, their efforts have been directed towards lawyers. Very little has been written for the benefit of the public at large and particularly those who will, sooner or later, become immersed in the intricacies of the law in areas which eventually few can avoid - not least Inheritance and Succession, related property rights and obligations, problems in family law and other topics which have a personal bearing on life.

John G. Murphy and Jason Dunne, who have a wealth of experience as solicitors, encouraged by their editor, Michael Freeman, have set about the provision of good advice for the laity in the foregoing crucial areas. It is not easy to open up the intricacies of the law in language which is not only readily understandable by non-lawyers, but also helps them to approach their particular problems in an atmosphere of sound common sense. That is a concept which the authors have skilfully achieved and in so doing have added a dimension of particular value for lay persons. I note that the authors have also devoted much thought to the importance of will-making; testamentary law and related problems, including the rights of spouses and children in that area.

A traditional difficulty in Irish life is that many people postpone testamentary action until the approach of death dictates that time is running out. Many inappropriate decisions on property dispositions after death and such matters have emerged on that account. It is right to advise people that it is most desirable to make their wills when in good health and when capable of deciding how best to perform that task in the interest of families and other intended beneficiaries. Testamentary litigation can be very expensive and potential grounds for it ought to be avoided. Thoughtful chapters on family law, taxation and problems relating to care of the elderly are also provided. These are topics of some difficulty which are becoming progressively more significant.

All-in-all, the end result is that the authors have provided the public with an admirable service in not only introducing them to aspects of law which are or will become of importance to many, but in doing so in a way which is full of good practical advice that prepares them for achieving maximum value from employment of a solicitor in due course. It is a particular pleasure to endorse what they have done.

- Mr. Justice Robert Barr

CONTENTS

LIFE

You may let your life happen or you may plan it. Better to have a plan than no plan. Otherwise, everyone else will take control of your life and that of your wife / husband / partner / children too.

A life plan is made up of mini plans that should all point towards a major plan that achieves less stress and worry and greater happiness and satisfaction.

Wealth creation and wealth management are all part of life planning.

Creating a Life Plan
Baby to 100 plus

The meaning of life has occupied religious leaders, philosophers, poets, anthropologists, sociologists, scientists, thinkers and writers for centuries.

Medical experts are forever trying to prolong life. Good politicians and economists focus on increasing our quality of life and our standard of living.

Some say that if managed properly, we all have the capacity to live to be 120. If you wish, aim for that. The average life expectancy of people in Ireland is about 80. That's only an average as some people live beyond 100.

Seasons of the Year
Your life span may depend on your genetic make-up, your nutrition, your food intake, and your life experiences in childhood, school, growing up, work, relationships, your posture, your physical exercise, your psychological make-up, your indomitable spirit and the level of your optimism for living life to the full.

Whatever philosophy or religious belief or experience you have, life generally follows a series of patterns or cycles just like the seasons of the year and just like economic, business and political

'Live life to the full'

'Eat, drink and be merry, and
don't worry about tomorrow'

' Earn, make, save, be resourceful
and give 10% to a good cause'

'Do your best as you know how'

'Go the extra mile'

' Live in day-tight compartments'

'Saw (the wood) hard but sharpen
the saw often'

'Carpe Diem (Seize the day)'

'Live life, love your family and
leave a good legacy '.

cycles or seasons. Ups and downs, downs and ups, like the rapids in a river at one time and like a calm, still pond at another. A few people have no ups or downs. Life is a charmed existence for them - a beautiful still pond on which the sun shines all the time. Imagine your own perfect life plan. From it develop your own inheritance and succession plan.

Quality of Life Check List

This simple quality of life check list may give you a sense of values that will guide your thinking and feelings.

Mind

- Are you happy? Happiness, like many of the other descriptions given below has many relative meanings. Answer the question according to your understanding of the word.
- Name three good things about yourself.
- Name three bad things about yourself.
- Do you have any black feelings or bad days?
- Would it help to discuss these with a trusted friend or professional?

Body

- Do you take exercise?
- Write down the days in the last week on which you did physical exercise and exactly how much time you took. The cumulative beneficial effect of regular, even gentle, exercise is huge. Consistency and continuity over a long time count.

Work / Business

- Are you happy with your work?
- Are you happy with your employer?
- Would you like to renew your employment efforts? Write down three things you will do to give yourself a more efficient tomorrow.
- If you have tried to make the best of your employment and it's just not working out write down three things you will do in the next week to source alternative employment.

Personal and Spiritual

Spirituality can mean different things for different people. Most are aware that each of us is part of a bigger scheme of things. Whether or not you believe in a god, you will surely recognise that there are immense forces for good and not so good at play.

Bring your mind regularly to a place where it can relax. Some achieve this through sport or exercise or just doing a hobby which they enjoy. Variety is important. All work and no play can make Jack or Jill very dull.

If you find your mind racing all the time and are always concerned about going faster while feeling less able to cope, try meditation to help you train your mind to be calm. Many people meditate to achieve peace and calmness. A simple prayer or a mantra can ease tensions and bring consolation and relaxation.

A Life Plan

Here is an ideal-type life cycle from the age of zero to get you thinking. Create your own ideal life plan with its cycles if you can.

LIFE PLAN

Baby-5 Every child should have the warmth and total security of parental love.

5-10   Children in this age group are developing personality, behaviour, temperament, basic life skills, forming friendships, exploring and learning to respect others.

10-15   Once young children, now starting to fly the nest. Becoming more adventurous. So much to learn. Keep the fun. Get involved in games, sports, walk in the country, on a beach or in a park. Get out there.

15-20   Between 15 and 20 can be rollercoaster years. Teenagers should respect themselves and respect others. Excessive use of alcohol and of drugs destroys or damages life.

20-30   These years go very fast. Take stock once a year. Just get a sheet of paper and scribble down things about what you are doing and what you'd like to achieve.

If staying solo or single, don't burn the candle at both ends. Strive for a work and life balance.

Marriage, having children, building a home, growing a business, wealth creation, developing your career or all of these may be your preoccupation from your mid 20s to your early 30s.

Marriage as an end in itself probably won't work. It is the most intimate contract you will ever make. This means that it needs work, your work, on a daily basis, to keep it going and growing. It doesn't mean you are joined at the hip for life. Keep up your separate interests from your wife / husband. Keep your mutually exclusive interests while also doing things together.

Children will change your life. Embrace the change. Enjoy it and be the best you can be at being a parent.

Don't just watch children grow. Get stuck in and help them grow. It's much more fun than the gym. Plan to do things together. Talk, think out loud, brainstorm, walk, share, go to a match, kick a ball around and talk as you go.

Guidenote: Shopping is not a means of communication or meaningful activity with children! Shopping is hard work.

Guidenote: You may decide that some of what you write or think of as your ideal life plan is nonsense. If you do, just cross that part out and look at the rest of it. Add something to it. The most important thing is that you keep on writing and amending your plans. Be careful - one day they may all come true.

30 - 40 Years of achievement and abundance when you and your family members have become self sufficient and independent. But still much more to be done.

40 - 60 For many people, the 40s and the 50s are a crossroads of change and emotion. For men and women it may be a mid-life crisis and feeling cheated of opportunity. Perhaps you have that depressing feeling that your life is going nowhere and that you should have done something else.

You may feel that perhaps you should have had a different partner, that you should have taken on a different job, that you should have done things differently.

You feel 'If only...' 'I would have...' Yesterday is gone, but you can use your experiences and education to change the future. Relax. Most people have similar feelings.

If these thoughts create a constant refrain in your head, stop being hard on yourself and beating yourself up. Identify something definite that you wish to do and that you can do. Then go for it. It is never too late. Acknowledge your achievements however small or big. Be positive. Select one or two things that you feel you should be doing, that you haven't been doing and that you will definitely do over the next week.

Here are some Simple Suggestions

1. When you go to your local shop or supermarket you probably just keep your head down, do your shopping hand over your money and go? Try this. Say hello to the cashier. Just like you, they are putting in their working day. Everyone likes a bit of light hearted banter or a chat or inspiration or just a friendly smile. But don't hold up the queue!

2. Do you have an elderly neighbour? Does that neighbour have good family or other back up? Try this. Call just to say Hello to that neighbour for just 10 minutes only or for a cup of tea or coffee. Stick to a 10 minutes visit but do it once a week.

3. Every GAA. rugby, soccer club or other sports club in Ireland needs an extra pair of hands on match days. You don't have to be a player and you don't have to be fit. Try this. Offer to sweep the dressing rooms or carry out the flags or count the jerseys. There is a bonus if you get to watch the match and you get to know a lot of new people.

4. Think of a friend who is in a similar situation to yourself and who you haven't spoken to for some time. Try this. Phone them and arrange to meet for a coffee, for a walk or discuss the idea of starting a book club, a discussion group, a new organisation or movement or a community activity. Become a revolutionary. Leave your footsteps in the sands of time.

60 - 70 The 60s are payback time. You have the right to enjoy a life and get a reward for doing so following your contribution big and small to the nation through the sweat of your brow. This time is your reward for doing so. Take every entitlement due to you. You have earned it.

Take all the physical exercise you can. If you have aches or pains get your doctor's advice early. Take an active interest with your doctor on the source of the pain. If you feel that you are 'just another patient' go to another doctor and get a second opinion.

Some people manage to organise a routine with which they are comfortable. This routine may include exercise, meeting friends, going to church, visiting family, continuing with work and so on. There are many however who may not be in the structured work force, or the family may be grown up or are leaving the nest. It can seem like a very empty time. Social experts have put a name on this phenomenon. You are an 'empty nester' !

A three word solution to this vacuum in your life is to BE NOT AFRAID. Fear of failure, fear of taking on something new, fear of rejection are all matters of the mind which stifle human endeavour.

So take that first bite. Sit down for 30 minutes with a check list today. Then put it to one side and take it out for 30 minutes again tomorrow. Start doing one or two new things that you can easily do. The key is: Get Started.

70 - 100 plus Gary Player the world famous golfer jogged up a mountain in South Africa and did sit ups and crunches in his 70s. He had exceptional physical talent. He worked at it and still worked at it in his 70s.

He did not do so to continue to be the world's number one golfer. He did it simply to keep himself in shape in order to get as much as possible out of life.

We may have less physical talent than Gary Player. But each of us is unique. Realise that there is only one of you. That is what makes you important.

Every day, take regular exercise, keep contact with friends and maintain involvement with clubs or organisations, assisting younger members of your family or other families. Keep on going. Focus on quality of life and living and keeping pain free and worry-free.

A good philosophy will carry you the full distance right up to the inevitable big full stop.

'Time is more important than money' - Anon

'Age is mind over matter. If you don't mind, it doesn't matter.'

'Never go to bed list less.'
(Listless means without writing a to-do list of things to be done next day.)

Investment for Life
and Succession

This chapter does not aim to give advice on how to invest. It is merely a guide based on our experience. For advice on how to invest, make an appointment with a qualified financial adviser, investment adviser, broker, stockbroker or accountant.

Early in life you may have lots of cash and no investment. Later in life you may have built up lots of assets and have little cash. Later still you may have lots of assets, lots of cash and be too busy or too old to spend it.

A Game of Chess

Investment is in one sense like playing a game of chess. Do you move the king now or do you wait until your opponent has fewer moves. Do you call your mortgage broker, building society or bank and invest in property by buying a house now or do you call your stockbroker and invest in equities or commodities. Do you save your money, and keep it all in a secure bank, credit union or post office? Do you use the return on your investment to reduce your mortgage?

A Cabbage Patch

In another way investment resembles growing a cabbage patch. Like investments, some cabbages will thrive and grow better than others, some cabbages will thrive at the expense of others that have been sown close by and some will not grow at all. Perhaps instead of having one big cabbage patch, divide it in two and grow some lettuce and carrots too!

A One Armed Bandit

And in another sense, investment may be like going to an amusement arcade and operating the one armed bandit on an impulse of buy, hold or sell. Buy an investment now, hold it until the market improves and then sell. Make a 'killing' and buy another investment without hopefully losing what you have made on the 'killing'! What you don't want right now may be somebody else's dream.

Investment in property and in equities has been shown over the long term of 10 years to 20 years to have outperformed other investments. Some people invest in just the top ten performing PLC companies on the stock exchange. Others invest in commodities.

Diversification, patience, a cool head and compound interest are said by most experts to be the keys to good returns on your investments.

Half Worry

Half of all people in Ireland are either continually concerned or very worried about money and about their future.

Their battle ranges between what they can afford to pay for day to day cost of living, how to keep their standard of living and quality of life, how to make repayments on borrowings or mortgages and at the same time how much to invest for their future. How can you really estimate how an investment is going to work out to give you more security for your years ahead and for your inheritance and succession plans?

It's best to aim at something rather than nothing. Smart people, guided by their investment or financial advisers, know when to take advantage of the ups and downs of economic cycles, market trends and investment returns.

They also know how to live life without being too tight and thrifty. And they know how to invest so that good returns will kick in at strategic times of their life such as when they buy a home, get married, children need funds, car needs to be replaced, house needs to be updated, new wardrobe is needed, go on a long holiday at 40, 50, 60, 70, 80, 90, 100 and so on. They also leave something for the rainy day or if they lose their job or face a crisis.

Parallel Plans
Working in parallel with their investment plans, progressive business people and farmers in particular make good succession plans.

An example is:
'At 40, I will give some responsibility in the company or farm to my son or daughter, nephew or niece or friend. At 50, I will send them on a training course for a year. At 55, I will give them control while I remain as managing director or chairman of the board and at 60 when my pensions kick into place, I will give them total control and get on with the rest of my natural life here on earth.'

Secret is Giving
Depending on our values, we should consider when we have more than enough to give some of that surplus to a worthwhile cause. George Samuel Clason, author of the world classic *The Richest Man in Babylon,* who has interesting observations on debt reduction and capital building suggests that part of the secret of living is giving!

Guidenote:Your circumstances today may not be your circumstances tomorrow. The law changes and so does tax legislation. It is up to you to review your will and you should do so regularly. Whether your will needs to be changed or not, it is worthwhile to review it at least every few years.

'It's all in the mind. John Milton said that the mind is its own place,

and in itself can make heaven of hell, and a hell of heaven'

A basic Investment to Succession to Inheritance Time Plan

PARENT'S AGE	INVESTMENT PLAN	SUCCESSION PLAN	INHERITANCE PLAN
20	College / Career Job / Fun / Marriage / Partners / Save for House / Invest in Pension		Make a Will.
25	Put some money into your own investment plan and in a saving plan for children.		Review your will.
30	Adjust your investment plan to give returns when you are 35, 40, 45 etc		
35	Update your investment plans to give returns when you are 40, 45, 50. Get advice on your pension plans.	Give some responsibility.	Review your will.
40	Review your investments and adjust them.		Review your will.
45	If you started investment plan at 20, you should now have exponential growth 25 years further down the road.	Give some control to successor. Seek commitment that someone will care for you at 70, 80, 90 etc.	
50	Review investments / pension	Give more control. Do an Enduring Power of Attorney.	
55	Review investments / pension	Take a back seat. Retire or Change Give increased control and involvement	Do an Enduring Power of Attorney.
60	Investments now provide serious return.		Review your will.

Wealth Management

Wise old Solomon would be confounded.

How do you hold onto what you have, preserve it, use it to grow more, become debt free, manage a mountain of paperwork, become financially independent, provide for your later years and leave a legacy to be enjoyed by your family or friends? Do you want to get rich or just get by?

Wise old Solomon would be perplexed.

Do you hold onto your house and your investments to make provision for your senior times? Do you hand your house and your investments over to your son, daughter, niece or nephew son in law, daughter-in-law, or a friend who will be able to make more of your estate?

Can you trust your advisers to ensure that you will be well insulated against recession, inflation and so on into your later years?

Building your Wealth

If you have assets of any kind you should consider managing them and directing them under your own wealth management plan or wealth management philosophy.

Such a plan or philosophy might be to:
- Use every possible asset in your list of assets.
- Avoid paying as much tax as possible.
- Take advantage of the benefits of investing in pension plans.
- Insure against loss.
- Build a diversified investment portfolio that will spread risk and enhance the chances of having a worry free retirement.
- Release equity safely from your home and so on.

You can't call on old Solomon as he died about two thousand years ago but you can call on the collective wisdom of an accountant, solicitor, bank, estate agent investment adviser, mortgage broker and insurance broker. Check if your financial advisers are regulated by the Financial Regulator.

The protection of wealth is as important as building wealth.

The word 'ask' is one of the most powerful in the English language, yet it has only three letters. There are no such things as silly questions. There are only silly answers. So Ask.

Ask

- your BANK for the balances on your bank accounts. You may have more / less than you think.

- your ACCOUNTANT for possible tax breaks, social welfare allowances and so on. You may be missing out or losing money unnecessarily.

- your INVESTMENT ADVISER for a list of your investments, whether cash, stocks, equities, property, collectibles, commodities, fine art, prize bonds and their value. You could be surprised.

- your ESTATE AGENT / AUCTIONEER / VALUER for a valuation of your home and property investment. Could be less or greater than you thought.

- your PENSION provider for an update on your pension. You may need to boost it.

- your INSURANCE BROKER for an estimate of the insurance cover on your estate. You may not have enough cover or you may have too much.

Consider Even if you are in debt, if you have any assets hold on to them for as long as you can. Over the long term, the capital gain on good assets should outstrip inflation and your repayments.

Consider If you sell assets such as your home or land, they are gone forever. Unless you have very deep pockets, you may not be able to get them back. It may be possible to release equity from a home or cash in an investment policy or even sell the car to pay off short term debts. Then your adviser can restructure your finances and off you go again.

Think

When doing your wealth management plan or your inheritance and succession plan, ask yourself:

- Can I gift some of my estate to children now while I am alive?
- Are gifts liable to inheritance tax?
- Is there advantage for me in setting up a limited company to avail of limited liability or tax incentives?
- Would it help if I transferred some of my assets overseas?
- Can I set up a Discretionary Trust?
- What happens if one of the members of the trust refuses to agree with the other members?
- Are there any tax allowances, reliefs that I may be entitled to?
- How long can I defer payment of taxes?
- Can I offset losses against capital gains tax?
- If I sell my house and move to another area, how long before I become liable to capital gains tax?

Do

First, take out your pen or pencil and a sheet of paper or open a spreadsheet on your PC and write down a list of your assets.

Second, write down a list of your liabilities. Subtract one from the other to find your present net worth.

Third, pick up the phone and make an appointment with your professional advisers, starting with your accountant and solicitor.

To plan your wealth protection may require advice from a host of specialists including your solicitor.

Governments introduce taxes to create incentives for investment and to pay for public services and social welfare. Avail of every tax allowance possible. The Revenue earn millions from people who don't claim what they're entitled to.

Avail similarly of social welfare allowances. You have probably paid for them hundreds of times anyhow in your lifetime of work or business.

When you are drafting your will, look at your present assets and liabilities and consider how tax burdens on beneficiaries may be avoided.

WHERE DO YOU STAND?

An example:

Assets

Home	€300,000
Furniture	€2,000
Land (a site)	€100,000
Investment property	€150,000
Car	€20,000
	€572,000

Liabilities

Overdraft in Bank	€10,000
Mortgages Per year	€100,000
	€110,000
Net assets (net worth)	€462,000

Regular Income

€500 per week	
Annual Total	€26,000

Regular Spending

Mortgage or rent	€10,000
Utilities-telephone, mobile phone	€1,000
Food	€4,000
Clothes	€2,000
Insurance	€1,000
Entertainment	€2,000
Total	€20, 000
Excess/ Shortfall	€6,000

Now having done your list, you'll be ready to face your adviser. Your request might be: 'Could you do a plan for me so that I might hold onto what I have, preserve it, use it to grow more, provide for my later years, become debt free and financially independent, draft a inheritance and succession plans and leave a legacy to be enjoyed by my family and friends when I cross over to the other side?'

Structure Finances

Your adviser may not have the wisdom of Solomon. However he/she may be able to structure your finances so that you can get your full tax allowances and social welfare allowances that you have paid for all your life through your taxes.

Perhaps your adviser can guide you towards investment, safe use of equity from your property, advise you on what shares you might keep and might sell, how to restructure your mortgage, take advantage of pensions schemes, rid yourself of your debts and project forward so that you become financially independent and make provision for your care for your later years. You may even have a legacy left over for loved ones to enjoy when you have passed on.

If you haven't already done so, right now call your accountant, solicitor, investment adviser asking for an appointment at his/her office or at your own home. You'll be doing yourself a favour. There's no feeling like peace of mind and knowing that you are moving forward.

Estate = property, investments, savings whether in bank or otherwise. In other words, it's the sum total of all your assets minus your liabilities.

Beneficiaries from Overseas

If you are a beneficiary living in Ireland, the solicitor will ask for your PPS number which goes something like 19999999 S or SW. If you are resident in the UK, you will be asked for your National Insurance number. This applies too if you are resident in other European countries.

Ireland and the UK have a common area agreement where tax matters are inter-linked. Inheritance Tax can be paid to the Revenue Commissioners in Ireland or to HM Customs and Revenue (Inland Revenue) in the UK. Usually the tax is paid in the country of source. Talk to your accountant or solicitor about your tax liabilities and especially Inheritance Tax and Capital Acquisitions Tax if any.

Building up your Pension and Investments

How would you like to be carefree, boss free, go as you please every day, have three long holidays and a cruise every year for the rest of your natural life after 50 while you get to live on the return from your investments paid directly into your bank or post office every month?

Meanwhile, you get to preserve your existing wealth, preserve your own inheritance, allow yourself to keep your children burden-free of looking after you in your old age and pass on some joy to your successors.

You may be able to afford it all if you have planned your investments and your pension. The word 'pension' which is really an old term for periodic payments means different things to different people and is used interchangeably. However it still has connotations of old age at a time when many people are retiring at age 45 and many more are working until they are 80.

Pension

It is never too early to start a pension and the sooner you start the better. Start your pension as soon as you start your first job in your teens or 20's.

The reason is simple. There is only a limited span of time for you to fund a pension and at the far end you are limited usually to age 65. If therefore you don't start until you are aged 35 the maximum number of years for you which you can fund the pension is 30 years instead of 45 years. You can't stretch it out beyond 65 and so the only solution is to start it early. This can make a huge difference.

In the past 15 years, Ireland has seen an extraordinary run of increasing property values. It was to a certain extent a catch up on values seen in other European countries and the realisation that we are as good as any of them. It also ran on a little over enthusiastically and like all good things it had to come to an end. Corrections are part of economic and financial cycles. We hope that few people will be over exposed to negative equity or debt.

It is most important to discuss the idea of investment with a trusted advisor such as an accountant, solicitor or stock broker. Get as many opinions as you can. Then evaluate the various opinions and make your decision.

Be cautious. It's your money. You can be lucky on following one particular asset but the wisdom of the ages is to keep a diversified portfolio of investments. This means that instead of buying three houses and having tenants, buy one house and put tenants in, buy some shares, put some money into a managed fund (low to medium risk perhaps) and keep some cash free for emergencies. The managed fund referred to can of course be your pension fund.

Wealth / Assets Protection

The greatest protector of your assets should be yourself. However, most of us are too busy to keep an eye on or manage our assets, expenses or cashflow.

The harsh reality is that many of us are financially irresponsible. A good and trustworthy bookkeeper and accountant will keep you on top of your business and investments. Remember whose business and investment it is. Verify and check and discuss all information extracted.

If your investments are at a level where you can't afford to pay a bookkeeper or accountant to monitor them, buy a notebook and write down in simple figures the value of assets and when you bought them, what they are worth now and what return or dividend or perhaps rent you are receiving every year. That will show your yield, i.e. the percentage being earned on your capital.

It is essential that you keep your taxes up to date and that you disclose to the revenue commissioners any rental income against which you can offset expenditure and borrowings interest.

There is nothing worse than getting a late penalty from the taxman where you have forgotten to pay tax and you will then not only have to pay the tax but also interest at a rate of about 12% per annum. To add insult to injury, penalties can be up to 75% of the tax liability.

Life Assurance

If you are young, married with a family and working, take out Life Assurance cover. It is cheap for a young person to do so and you can provide a substantial lump sum for your family in the event of your untimely death.

Do you know what level of cover you actually need?

Here is a warning. There are some unscrupulous brokers at large who will try to sell all kinds of add-ons to basic life assurance cover. Do you know the level of cover that you need?

Critical illness cover, permanent health insurance and loss of employment insurance is available. Ask about the different levels of cover available so that you will know the precise cost to you.

In one case some years ago, a small business owner put €35,000 into a policy over a period of three years and found that the amounts leaving his bank account were increasing every year.

With his accountant and solicitor he investigated the matter and discovered that while he had paid out €35,000 over three years, the insurance company had received €20,000 and the broker had received €15,000 of his money. It is now more reassuring that the Financial Regulator has mechanisms to protect people from this behaviour.

The paperwork issued by some insurance companies for sales of life assurance or critical illness or savings products is cumbersome. The reality is that most people don't read it or can't read it or don't understand it.

One solution is to offer clients a simple response sheet completed as follows:
1. Annually you will pay a total of €...
2. The insurance/life assurance company will receive a total of €...
3. Your broker (Mr/Ms ....) will receive a total of €...

The regulators could do well to request insurance companies to supply the answers to these questions to their clients as a requirement of sales.

In real money terms, what are you worth? You are so busy at your every day life, you haven't time to think about it let alone do some planning.

We hope the following examples will help :

1. You are reasonably well off but a bit uncertain

A. Make an appointment with a good accountant. Ask for a statement of your net worth and also your income and expenditure.

Then follow the advice and go and get all the information asked for. Before you leave his or her office, make the next appointment. With guidance and a little effort, you will soon have a clear picture of where you are in terms of assets, income and expenditure.

B. The next phase will be to assess if:
    (a) you should sell any asset or raise money to do something new.
    (b) you can reduce any unnecessary expense.
    (c) you can improve your income by re-organising your work.

C. Then do it, make the changes.

2. Money is Tight
    You feel you can't afford to pay an accountant? Try to negotiate a reasonable price.
    If you still feel you can't afford it, then get stuck in and do it yourself.
A. Write an Asset/Liability list
B. Write an Income/Expenditure list
C. Is there any Asset to sell so you could use the proceeds more effectively? If you think
    so, take some professional advice first. If the advisor seems a little too keen on getting
    the sale going rather than giving you all the options, you are in the wrong place!
    (a) Can you reduce any of the expenditure on the list?
    (b) Can you improve your income?
    (c) Go to your Citizens Information office to check if there are any Social Welfare or
        Family Income Supplements to which you might be entitled.
        It's free, at least go in and ask.
    (d) If debts are a worry, contact and go and see the Money Advice Bureau (MABS).
        Again, it's free and its officials are very experienced in dealing with difficult debt
        situations. It can relieve a lot of worry to share your burden with someone who
        can actually assist.

CHECK YOUR ASSETS
Aged 20 – 40

House
If you do not already own a house buy one if you can. Its asset value comes into play much
later in your life.

Investment Property
Consider buying an investment property if you can afford it. Even with a current
downturn in housing values, a well built house in a good location (particularly at a
discount) should still be a good long term investment. Can you afford the mortgage if you
only have tenants for say, nine months of the year? Be realistic and prudent in estimating
rental income and costs of upkeep.

Holiday Home Abroad
Consider carefully whether a holiday home abroad is a good investment. If you need to rent

it so that it pays for itself, will you be happy arriving there for your holiday looking at damage caused by tenant's ordinary use or possibly worse? Do you really want to go to the same place for holidays every year? Stand back and look at it in real investment terms.

Shares

Do you really know anything about the companies listed on the stockmarket? Most people know very little about the stock market. So only invest in the blue chip companies if you don't have time to watch the market. Buy small amounts over time and keep an eye on what's happening. If you have time to research and keep in touch regularly with a good stockbroker, you can be a little more adventurous. Ask the stockbroker to put a 'stop-loss' in place.

Managed Funds (for a lump sum investment)

Consider managed funds for a minimum of five years investment, preferably ten years, otherwise you may lose out. Check the last twenty year history of the company managing your fund. Before you write the cheque, ask how much exactly the company will take from your money every year in charges or fees or commissions. Get this in writing in a straight forward, short letter from the broker or company. It is very difficult to find the answer in the ridiculous amount of paperwork thrown at you by insurance companies.

Pension

Get into a pension the minute you start your first job. That's all – do it! If you move jobs, sometimes the pensions can't be moved and will be frozen so whatever you have in it will be protected. Some pensions can be moved, but it always depends on the type of pension you have and the way it is set up. Check with your employer or the pension provider directly.

Cash

Always keep some cash aside, just for emergencies. Get the best rate you can. It's good to have a good relationship with your bank. Check interest rates on deposits of other banks and ask your bank manager to match them.

Aged 40 – 60

Ideally this is a time to consolidate investments. Make sure you hold what you have but also avail of any investment / pension opportunities that present themselves. Consider AVCs. They are a good means of building your pension fund.

Maybe do a top up into your pension but take a closer interest in your shareholdings. Constantly revise your work / life balance.

Aged 60 plus

Retirement beckons. Continue to appraise your position. Unless you are used to it, it is not a time to take risks.

'If an investment seems to be too good to be true,
then it probably is.'

'According to a study in the US , less than 10% of worries
are worth doing anything about.'

My Assets

Some people may think they have little or nothing. Sit down and do a list. You may be simply amazed at what you have when you write it out.

Work through the following list as a guide whether you are planning succession, retirement or inheritance.

House

Do you own your home? If so, you own a very valuable asset. Who holds the deeds? Are they held by your bank? Are they held by your solicitor? Do you have the deeds?

House Contents

Do you have expensive furniture? While some people will have flat pack items, others have the best leather furniture, solid oak tables and so on. Sometimes when a person dies and their house is being sold, the contents of the house are sold also and in some cases the contents which may include some quality furniture can be worth a lot of money.

Land

Do you own any land? Even with the recent downturn in the economy, land is still a very valuable commodity. There is only so much of it to go around. Who has the deeds?

Investment Property

Do you have a house that you rent out? Do you own a holiday home? During the boom some people invested in the property market and bought a property to rent. Many Irish people bought a house in Spain, Portugal, France, Bulgaria, USA or South Africa.

Do you have a solicitor or lawyer in that country? Do they have the deeds or are those deeds with a bank or building society? You should have a separate will for that foreign asset because the law there may be different from our laws.

Interest in Expectancy

Not everyone will have an 'interest in expectancy'. For example if your father leaves the family farm to your mother for her lifetime and after her death it is left to you, you have an interest in expectancy. Basically you will be taking the farm from your father but you will only get it when your mother dies.

Bank / Building Society - Current Account / Deposit Account / Savings Account

Almost everyone has an account with a bank or building society. Some people have numerous accounts in one bank. Some have several accounts in several banks. Many parents nowadays will open an account when a child is born. Who has the deposit book?

Credit Union

A great number of people now have a credit union account. When you open an account with a credit union you become a member, as opposed to customer, of that branch. Credit Unions provide a convenient way to save and borrow. If you have a loan outstanding when you die, the credit union have you insured, provided you are under 70 when you join, so the debt is usually repaid by the insurance.

Unlike a bank or building society account, you can nominate the proceeds of the account to a person after your death. If you are unsure whether your account is nominated or not, contact your branch. They usually give the information over the phone. The nominee you have chosen gets the fund(to a max of €23,000). It is not dealt with under your will. Also if you have made a nomination and then get married, the marriage revokes the nomination.

Post Office

Do you have a Post Office account or saving bonds? Savings bonds are state guaranteed and many people prefer them as a method of saving.

Prize Bonds

Do you have Prize Bonds? Many people have them and don't even know it. They may have inherited them from a parent or relative and promptly forgotten all about them. They are sometimes given as a gift instead of money. They are State guaranteed and are entered into a draw every month. Where are the original bonds located?

Cars / Boats / Motorcycles

People as young as 17 now have a car or motorcycle. Some use it to commute to work. Some use it for leisure. Some use it just to get from A to B. Others may have classic cars. Depending on the make and model and how well they are looked after, classic cars will appreciate in value over time. You may have a small two-man fishing boat…

Stocks / Shares / Gold

Do you have shares in telecoms, insurance companies or banks? You may be playing the stock market and have built up a decent portfolio. You may have invested in gold or other commodities.

Whatever type of share or stock you have be sure to keep the original certificates in a safe place and keep a record of them.

Pensions / PRSA / State

Do you have a pension for your retirement either private or State? Check the terms of it. Will it be payable only on retirement or will it be worth something on your death?

If you've been a net contributor all your life and have paid your PAYE you will be entitled to a contributory pension at 65.

ERS or EU retirement schemes are important to farmers and facilitate early retirement from farming, usually at age 55. Are you in such a scheme?

Life Insurance / Assurance

Have you got an insurance policy or an assurance policy? Some policies are payable on death. Some are for a set term of years, after which you receive a lump sum. If it's for death cover only, you personally will get nothing.

Tell your solicitor where the original documents are located. Check to see if the proceeds of the policy or policies are nominated to anyone in the event of your death. If they are, they will not be dealt with under your will.

Antiques / Art / Wine / Heirlooms

More and more people are investing in antiques, art, wine and heirlooms. Art is usually worth more when the artist dies, which is unfortunate for the artist! Antiques maintain their value and in many cases are worth more over time. Wines like people, are ever aging. Beware though as some will not age well. Some collectors will pay top dollar for rare bottles of good vintage.

Many families have heirlooms which sometimes are worth nothing but in some cases they can be of surprising value. These include stamps, coins, and that All-Ireland medal.

Jewellery

Diamond, ruby, emerald? Perhaps you have an expensive watch or necklace or maybe you have something that has sentimental value to a member of your family. Either way these items are of value. Make an inventory or list of your jewellery, especially if you have two items that are similar, that you wish to leave to different people. It avoids confusion later. We have seen a major estate become embroiled in years of litigation due to a row over the silver spoons.

Cash

Money talks.

DEBTS OR LIABILITIES

Most people have debts or liabilities. You may be in the happy situation of having none. However, if you have debts, manage them carefully or they may take over and manage you. Seek advice early if you have debt worries.

Mortgage

A mortgage can be cleared on your death by a life policy meaning your spouse or children or whoever you leave the house to, can take the house mortgage free. If you don't have a life policy then unfortunately your beneficiary will have to take over the mortgage or sell the asset to clear it off. Check with your bank, building society or other financial institution with whom you have your loan or mortgage.

Car Loan

Finance will typically be either a loan or a hire purchase agreement. With a loan you own the car and you repay the bank. With a hire purchase agreement or finance deal the car remains the property of the finance company until you repay the debt.

Overdraft

A lot of people live their daily lives in the red. However a bank overdraft can be a useful facility to manage cashflow without having to borrow long term. Check the interest rate and the amount of interest you are paying.

Credit Cards

Almost all of us have a credit card. If you pay it off in full and on time each month then it can be very useful and a good way to make purchases. However, more than half of us don't pay it off each month and so it becomes a niggling debt which can get out of hand pretty quickly.

Unfortunately, it's a debt that doesn't die with you, so if it still remains it will have to be paid from your estate. Interest rates on credit cards are usually very high. Shop around. Move your balance to a new card to avail of an interest free period or a better interest rate.

Conclusion

Add it all up. You're probably worth more than you thought, even after you take out the mortgage and the other debts. Have the list done out before you go to see your solicitor about your will. It will help the solicitor and it will help you.

Guidenote: Check the wording on your deeds for burdens and special conditions. Burdens include debts. These may be debts due by you or by a previous owner of your house or land. They may even be written on your deeds by mistake for example because of similarity of names. To remove burdens of debt due by you, you will have to pay to have them removed from your deeds.

Check your title deeds. Ask your solicitor to check them and ensure that they are in order.

My Personal Affairs
and Possessions List

My Personal Affairs and Possessions List is an important checklist which you should, regardless of your age, complete, sign and date and give to your solicitor for safe-keeping and for reference. Notify your executors and attorneys that you have completed the list and that you have given it to your solicitor.

You should give your executors and attorneys the name and contact details of your solicitor. In case of emergency, such as if you become incapacitated, this list will be a source of valuable information that will enable your representatives to manage your affairs. It can save time, effort and money in your solicitor's efforts to help you manage your affairs and respond to emergencies. It can also help save your life.

Put your Personal Affairs and Possessions List in a folder or on a disc or USB memory stick for your solicitor. If you are keeping a copy at home make sure to store it in a safe place. Be aware that identity theft is a major risk.

Using the following list as a guide, compile and type a list specific to your own requirements. For a download version please visit www.myinheritance.ie

EMERGENCIES

FOR EMERGENCIES, PLEASE CONTACT (INDICATING) MY PARTNER
(P), NEXT OF KIN (NOK), (HUSBAND, WIFE, AUNT, UNCLE,
BROTHER, SISTER, NEPHEW, NIECE, COUSIN AND SO ON), FRIEND
(F), NEIGHBOUR (N) AS FOLLOWS:

FULL NAME (NOK), (P)
TELEPHONE
MOBILE
HOME ADDRESS

BUSINESS ADDRESS

EMAIL:

FULL NAME (F)
TELEPHONE
MOBILE
HOME ADDRESS

BUSINESS ADDRESS

EMAIL:

FULL NAME (N)
TELEPHONE
MOBILE
HOME ADDRESS

BUSINESS ADDRESS

EMAIL

FULL NAME (N)
TELEPHONE
MOBILE
HOME ADDRESS

BUSINESS ADDRESS

EMAIL

MEDICAL

DOCTOR
FULL NAME
TELEPHONE
MOBILE

HOME ADDRESS

BUSINESS ADDRESS

EMAIL:

DENTAL

DENTIST
FULL NAME
TELEPHONE
MOBILE

HOME ADDRESS

BUSINESS ADDRESS

EMAIL:

MY BLOOD TYPE IS

LEGAL

MY PPS NUMBER / PENSION NUMBER IS:

SOLICITOR
FULL NAME
FIRM
TELEPHONE
MOBILE
BUSINESS ADDRESS

EMAIL: MY GRAVE IS AT:

EXECUTOR 1 - LEGAL PERSONAL REPRESENTATIVE
NAME
ADDRESS
                                                MORTAL REMAINS
                                                MY MORTAL REMAINS ARE TO BE INTERRED AT:
TEL
EMAIL

EXECUTOR 2
NAME   MY MORTAL REMAINS ARE TO BE CREMATED AND THEN
ADDRESS   INTERRED / SPREAD AT:

TEL
EMAIL

Attorney 1 (FOR ENDURING POWER OF ATTORNEY)   MY FUNERAL ARRANGEMENTS DOCUMENT IS LOCATED AT:
NAME
ADDRESS

                                                MY WILL IS STORED WITH:
TEL   NAME
                                                TEL:

Attorney 2 (FOR ENDURING POWER OF ATTORNEY)
NAME   THE LAST UPDATE OF MY WILL WAS ON DAY / MONTH / YEAR
ADDRESS

TEL   MY ORGANS ARE TO BE DONATED TO:

FUNERAL ARRANGEMENTS
FUNERAL DIRECTORS / UNDERTAKERS
NAME
ADDRESS   MY BODY IS TO BE DONATED FOR ANATOMICAL RESEARCH
                                                TO:

TEL

**LIST OF PEOPLE HERE AND OVERSEAS TO
BE NOTIFIED BY MY EXECUTORS OF MY DEATH:**

Names and address

Names and address

Names and address

Names and address

Names and address

THE DEEDS OF MY PROPERTY (IES) ARE HELD:
BY....

AT....

MY DOCUMENTS SAFE IS LOCATED AT:

SAFE CODES:

Misc. Codes:

PREMISES DOORS

COMPUTERS

STORAGE UNITS

KEYS LOCATED AT:

HOME

PREMISES

CAR KEYS

FINANCIAL
EMPLOYERS:
NAME
ADDRESS

TEL

BANK(S)
NAME
ADDRESS

TEL

BANK BRANCH AND SORT CODE

CREDIT CARD PROVIDER

INSURERS

NAME

ADDRESS

CREDIT CARD NUMBERS:

TEL

POLICY NUMBERS

MORTGAGE PROVIDER / BROKER:

MORTGAGE ACCOUNT NUMBER:

BUILDING INSURANCE

ACCOUNTANT

NAME

FIRM

CONTENTS INSURANCE

TELEPHONE

MOBILE

HOME ADDRESS

CAR INSURANCE

BUSINESS ADDRESS

EMAIL

FINANCIAL ADVISERS

ASSURANCE POLICIES

NAME

FIRM

TELEPHONE

MOBILE

HOME ADDRESS

PENSION

BUSINESS ADDRESS

PENSION FUND PROVIDER

NAME

ADDRESS

EMAIL

POLICY NUMBER

INTEREST IN EXPECTANCY

PENSION FUND PROVIDER

NAME

ADDRESS

BANK / BUILDING SOCIETY - CURRENT / DEPOSIT / SAVINGS

ADDRESSES

CREDIT UNION

POLICY NUMBER

POST OFFICE

COMPANY DIRECTORSHIPS

ESTATE AND ASSET LIST

HOUSE

PRIZE BONDS

CARS / BOATS / MOTORCYCLES

HOUSE CONTENTS

STOCKS / SHARES / GOLD

LAND

INVESTMENT PROPERTY

PENSIONS / PRSA / STATE

LIFE INSURANCE/ASSURANCE

OF .... CHURCH

SOCIAL AND PROFESSIONAL

MEMBERSHIPS OF ORGANISATIONS / ASSOCIATIONS:

ANTIQUES / ART / WINE / HEIRLOOMS

JEWELLERY

NAME(S) AND ADDRESS (ES) OF ORGANISATION/ASSOCIATION

CASH

MEMBERSHIPS OF PROFESSIONAL BODIES

RELIGIOUS

CLERGY

NAME(S) AND ADDRESS (ES) OF PROFESSIONAL BODIES.

MY PREFERRED CLERGY ARE

TAX

The taxman giveth or the taxman taketh away.

Taxes and duties are collected in order to provide funding for public services. There are many kinds of taxes and duties and no doubt most people will be familiar with the ones that can affect everyday life including Income tax, VAT and VRT. They may not be so familiar with the taxes that can impact on a gift or inheritance.

Thousands of euros may be lost through a lack of knowledge of not only the taxes but also the reliefs that can be claimed.

Up to 20% of your estate could be lost due to wrong decisions, poor planning or even just bad timing.

Minimising *Tax*

The Taxman may take 20% or one fifth of your estate if you are not careful in your inheritance and succession decisions. Much depends on your relationship to your beneficiary or beneficiaries and as such on their tax thresholds. It depends too on how you plan your tax.

When you die, your successors and beneficiaries may have to pay tax. Tax is a major driver in decision-making for succession and inheritance decisions.

Tax has a huge bearing on how much your estate will be worth in the future whether you give it as a gift, make it part of a succession plan or make a bequest to loved ones in an inheritance plan.

Don't be Daunted
But don't be daunted. Timely advice from a professional adviser when planning your inheritance or succession matters will enable you to legitimately and significantly reduce or even eliminate the tax bill altogether.

This chapter will alert you to the many exemptions, reliefs and deductions that are available.

The overall tax that we are mainly concerned about in inheritance and succession decisions comes under the heading of Capital Acquisitions Tax or in other words CAT.

CAT comprises a number of important taxes. These include:
Gift Tax, Inheritance Tax, Trust Tax and Probate Tax.

Gift Tax arises when a beneficiary receives a gift from a living person (called a donor or disponer).

Inheritance Tax arises when a beneficiary receives a benefit when someone dies.

Trust Tax arises where assets are put into a discretionary trust.
The trustees pay tax of 6% in the first year and then 1% per year.

Probate Tax abolished from December 2000, arises for deaths that have occurred between 18th June 1993 and 6th December 2000. It is still relevant for estates where the person died between those dates but whose estate is only now being administered.

Two other taxes to be considered are:

Capital Gains Tax which arises on the gain made in the value of the estate or property between the date of acquisition and sale or disposal. The tax to be paid is 20% of the value of the gain.

Stamp Duty, which is paid by a purchaser or a beneficiary on a gift of property, varies from 1% to 9%.

CAPITAL ACQUISITIONS TAX (CAT)

The idea of giving someone a gift either now or when you are gone would no doubt be warmly welcomed by your chosen beneficiary. What most people don't think about is that on giving a gift or inheritance, they may be burdening the beneficiary with a sizeable tax bill. The prospect of such a bill should force you if you are a donor to think not only about 'how' and 'when' but sometimes 'who' you decide to benefit either by way of gift or inheritance.

You may have worked hard all your life and paid your fair dues in taxes so you don't wish to see a large chunk of that going into the Government's coffers either whilst you are alive or after your death. As we said earlier, with guidance, some careful planning and a little foresight you may be able to legitimately eliminate or at least minimise taxes for your beneficiaries. So, whether you have a farm, lottery winnings, a portfolio of shares or even if you only have the roof over your head, you should plan ahead.

What are your family circumstances?
Are you married or do you have a life long partner?
Do you have children? If so, are they from a marital on non-marital relationship? Are the children adopted or fostered?

You may wish to make a gift of some of your estate to your loved ones now. Or you may decide to hang on to it and leave it in your will.

No matter how much or how little you have, you should decide what's going to happen to it either now or when you're gone and whether it can be passed on to your beneficiary or beneficiaries tax efficiently.

What is taxable?
Anything of value in the State and capable of being passed from one person to another is taxable. A car, money, land, a business, shares and so on.

Property outside the State for example in Spain or a shareholding in the UK may be taxable where either the disponer or the beneficiary is resident or ordinarily resident in Ireland.

For residency requirements see www.revenue.ie

When does the tax arise?
A tax arises at the 'valuation date', which is when you become "beneficially entitled in possession" to the item that has been given or left to you. These are revenue terms and basically they mean that you have received, or you are entitled to receive, or are already in possession of, the item.

For gifts, the valuation date will either be the date you receive the benefit or the date it is actually or legally transferred to you.

For inheritances, it can be the date of death of the person you are to receive it from or it can be the date of the Grant of Probate / Administration, which will be some months later.

If you are to receive something in the future then you have what is known as a 'future interest' and you will not be taxed on the item until you actually receive it.

But what does the valuation date really mean?
The valuation date is the date that determines when the tax, if any, becomes payable to the Revenue Commissioners. It is the earliest of the dates above on which you become 'beneficially entitled in possession' to the item you are receiving.

If there is a tax liability then it must be paid within four months of the valuation date.

How do you know if you have a tax liability?

If the gift or inheritance is passing through the hands of your solicitor then he or she will let you know as soon as possible if you have any tax to pay.

Your tax liability depends on your relationship to the disponer or testator and also on whether you have received any prior gifts or inheritances from someone in the same group threshold.

Who pays the tax?

The beneficiary usually pays the tax.

What if you pay something towards the gift or inheritance?

If you pay something towards the gift or inheritance, it is called 'consideration'. For example, your uncle wants to give you a house but he would like to get something from you for it without hitting you for what would be the full sale price or market value.

If the house is worth €300,000 but you pay him €100,000 towards it, then you are deemed to be receiving a gift of€€€200,000. The difference is the consideration you pay him for it. On the gift of €200,000, you will of course be liable for tax. Unless you qualify for any relief or exemption.

How much is the tax?

Tax is payable at 20% on everything over and above the threshold. Interest and penalties will apply on unpaid or overdue taxes. Interest is currently 0.0273% per day.

How is the tax paid?

The tax is paid by filling in an IT38 tax return form available from the Revenue by post or from their website. The form must be submitted to the Revenue and must be accompanied by the appropriate payment usually by cheque or bank draft.

Payments and returns can now be made online using the Revenue's online service (ROS), but you must register with Revenue to be able to avail of this service. Details on how to complete the form are contained in the IT39 explanatory leaflet, available on www.revenue.ie. Solicitors or accountants can do this also for you.

How much can you get before paying tax?

Beneficiaries are categorised into groups depending on their relationship to the disponer or testator. The groups are index linked to the consumer price index (CPI) so they rise annually with inflation.

The indexed Group thresholds for 2006, 2007 and 2008 are set out in the table below.

GROUP	RELATIONSHIP TO DISPONER	GROUP THRESHOLD 2006 (AFTER INDEXATION)	GROUP THRESHOLD 2007 (AFTER INDEXATION)	GROUP THRESHOLD 2008 (AFTER INDEXATION)
A	Son/Daughter	€478,155	€496,824	€521,208
B	Parent/Brother/Sister/ Niece/Nephew/Grandchild	€47,815	€49,682	€52,121
C	Relationship other than Group A or B	€23,908	€24,841	€26,060

Example:
A parent leaves an estate valued at €600,000 by will to a child. The threshold is €521,208. This leaves €78,792 (€600,000 – €521,208) to be taxed. Tax is 20% of €78,792. Therefore the tax is €15,758.40 which the child will have to take from the amount given, raise from own savings or resources or from borrowings such as a mortgage from a bank, building society or credit union loan to pay the tax to the Revenue.

Group A
€521,208
A child or a minor child of a pre-deceased child.
'Child' includes a step child or an adopted child (in accordance with the Adoption Acts).

A foster child will also qualify for group A threshold in respect of any benefit taken since December 2000 if they have been cared for and maintained up to the age of 18 and have resided with the disponer for at least five (5) years.

Parents, who would normally be in Group B but who take an absolute inheritance (as opposed to a gift) from a child, on the death of that child, will qualify for Group A relief. The relief provides for the unfortunate situation of a child dying before the parent.

Group B
€52,121
This group includes parents (where they are receiving a gift from a child) or grandparents, grandchildren or great grandchildren, brothers and sisters, nieces and nephews (although a niece or nephew related through marriage will not qualify).
My niece is my sister's child and so is truly my niece. My niece's husband, though he might refer to me as his uncle, is NOT my nephew.

It only applies to blood relatives. In-laws fall into Group C.

Group C
€26,060

This applies to everyone else, cousins, friends etc., that is anyone who doesn't fit into groups A or B. For tax purposes they are called 'strangers in blood'. In certain cases, a beneficiary can step into the shoes of his/her deceased spouse. For example, a daughter in law of the disponer, who would typically be in Group C, can qualify for the group A threshold (as opposed to group C) if her husband pre-deceased the disponer.

Grandchild or minor child of a predeceased child
If you leave a gift or inheritance to your child, but your child dies before you, leaving children of their own, then those children can each step into Group A and avail of the higher threshold to which their parent (your child) would have been entitled.

If you leave a gift or inheritance directly to your grand-child then they have a Group B threshold.

What about spouses?
Spouses are completely exempt from CAT.

AGGREGATION
Gifts or inheritances (benefits) within the same group threshold are aggregated for tax purposes. To aggregate means to add together any prior benefit that you received to the current benefit to see whether or not there is any present liability for tax.

Benefits received since 5th December 1991 will be taken into account but benefits received prior to that date are not aggregated.

Aggregation is best shown by an example:
Johnny gets a gift of €100,000 from his mother (Group A) in 1995. He then receives a gift of a classic car from his uncle (Group B) in 2005 worth €30,000 and then inherits an apartment from his father (Group A) in 2008 worth €300,000.

The gift from his mother and the inheritance from his father are aggregated as they are both from Group A disponers giving a combined total of €400,000. As Johnny is under his threshold for 2008, he pays no tax.

The Group B gift from his uncle is not aggregated with Group A, and as he does not exceed his (Group B) threshold for 2005 of €46,673, he pays no tax.

So, in 2008 you can receive €521,208 from a parent, €52,121 from an aunt and €26,060 from a friend and not pay any tax as none of them are aggregated.

RIGHT OF RESIDENCE OR LIFE INTEREST

Remember, a benefit is only taxable when the beneficiary is entitled to have or to receive it. For example, your uncle dies and leaves his house to you but gives his wife an exclusive right to reside in the house for her lifetime. What are the tax implications?

First you are receiving the legal title to the house but as you have no beneficial interest in it there is no immediate tax. Your aunt is not taxed on the right of residence as there is no tax between spouses. On the death of your aunt you are deemed to receive your uncle's house and you will have four months from that date within which to pay any tax arising.

The same is true of a life interest. In this case, your uncle leaves his house to his wife for her lifetime and when she dies, you will get it. Here your aunt has a life interest in the house. As they are spouses, she pays no tax on that interest. You only have a future interest in the house so you pay no tax at that time. You will get the house from your uncle but only when your aunt dies. You pay tax at that stage.

Trust Tax

Trusts are covered in a later chapter but are mentioned here just to let you know that they are taxable. Trusts are usually set up to provide for children under 18 or perhaps for a child suffering from a severe mental or physical disability. (See Other Exemptions and Reliefs from CAT on page 64)

CAT is payable where the beneficiary exceeds their threshold.
However where a discretionary trust is set up trust tax may also arise. The tax is payable at 6% and is a once off payment. It can be reduced to 3% if the trust is fully wound up within 5 years. There is also an annual tax payable of 1% over the life of the trust. If all assets in the trust are distributed before the youngest beneficiary reaches 21, no tax is payable by the trust.

With careful planning a discretionary trust can be very useful both from a legal and a tax perspective, especially where young children are concerned.

Probate Tax

Probate Tax was introduced by the Finance Act 1993 and was subsequently abolished by the Finance Act 2001. It is still relevant however if a person died in say 1994 but their estate is only now being administered.

The tax is charged at the rate of 2% on the estates of persons dying on or after 18 June 1993 and before 6 December 2000. For deaths occurring on or after 18 June 1993 and before 6th December 1999 a charge to Probate Tax arose if the deceased was domiciled in Ireland at date of death or resident from 1999 to 2000, or if the estate included Irish assets.

EXEMPTIONS RELIEFS AND DEDUCTIONS FROM CAT

Spouses
Gifts or inheritances taken by a spouse from a spouse are entirely exempt from CAT, regardless of the amount involved. Transfers of property between spouses following a divorce can be exempt from CAT provided the transfer is completed in accordance with the terms of the divorce.

Proposals have been made to give gay couples and qualifying cohabitants a similar exemption. However nothing has been enacted at time of writing.

Liabilities, Costs and Expenses
Before arriving at a taxable figure, certain deductions can be made. These deductions include stamp duty and legal fees where the beneficiary receives a gift. In the case of an inheritance, it includes legal fees, funeral expenses or any debts owed by a deceased person prior to his/her death. So don't feel too bad about those legal fees as they reduce your tax.

Annual Exemption
The annual exemption applies to a gift only i.e., between living persons and does not apply to an inheritance. At the moment the annual exemption is €3,000. Therefore the first €3,000 of the taxable value of any gift is exempt from CAT. A beneficiary can receive gifts from the same disponer in different calendar years and the first €3,000 of each gift will be exempt from tax. Also, a beneficiary can take gifts from numerous different disponers in the same year and the first €3,000 of each gift will be exempt. You can add this to your threshold.

Example
John receives a gift today from his brother Michael of €3,000. This is exempt from tax. Later the same year, John can receive a further full threshold amount from his brother of €52,121 without paying any tax.

AGRICULTURAL RELIEF
What is agricultural property?
Agricultural property can be agricultural land, pasture and woodland in the State with crops, trees and underwood growing on the land.

Houses and other farm buildings appropriate to the property, livestock, bloodstock and farm machinery and entitlements (single payment) are all deemed to be agricultural assets.

Be aware: "Entitlements" will only be classed as agricultural assets where they are passed with land to a beneficiary. Entitlements are rights built up on land by production. These rights entitle you to the EU Single Payment each year.

To qualify for agricultural relief the gift or inheritance must consist of agricultural property both at the date of the gift or inheritance and at the valuation date.

What is a Farmer?

You can be a farmer for tax purposes but you don't actually have to be farming. It has nothing to do with your occupation. You must simply be an individual (a company cannot be a farmer), be resident in the State and at least 80% of the gross market value of your assets are represented on the valuation date by agricultural property after taking the gift or inheritance into account.

The 'Farmer test' is a Revenue test designed to establish whether or not a person is a farmer for tax purposes. The pass mark is 80% and once a beneficiary's agricultural assets total 80% or more of all of his assets, then he will pass the test and qualify for agricultural relief. The farmer percentage test and the residency requirement are not necessary in respect of trees and underwood.

If you qualify for it, this can be a major relief from CAT. It reduces the market value of the agricultural assets being received in the gift or inheritance by 90%. So a farm that is valued at €1,000,000 is reduced in value by 90% to €100,000 for tax purposes. Liabilities on the farm such as a mortgage are ignored i.e., they are not taken into account.

However since 2007 any mortgage on the off-farm residence, which would typically be your own house, can be taken into account, i.e., only the value of the house, less the mortgage, will be used thus giving you a small non-agricultural asset figure.

In order to qualify for the relief you must be deemed to be a farmer on the valuation date and to establish whether you are a farmer or not a simple test involving a calculation of your assets must be carried out.

For example: Sean was left a 200 acre farm in Meath, stock, machinery and entitlements in his father's will. It is worth say, €4,000,000. Sean's threshold in 2008 is €521,208 and he received no prior gifts or inheritances. Sean has his own house worth €200,000 and €4,000 in the bank. Using these figures we apply the test using the following criteria to see whether or not he qualifies as a farmer:

Total assets are €4,204,000. You must then divide the agricultural value of €4,000,000 by the total assets of €4,204,000 which gives a figure of 0.9514 and this is multiplied by 100 to get the percentage value, i.e. 95.14%, which means he exceeds the 80% requirement,

An example of the 80% Test

ASSET	AGRICULTURAL	NON- AGRICULTURAL
Farm, stock etc	€4,000,000	-
House	-	€200,000
Bank	-	€4,000
Totals	€4,000,000	€204,000

qualifies as a farmer, and can avail of agricultural relief. If he didn't get agricultural relief he would pay tax on €3.5m at 20%.

The savings are simply huge. The market value of the farm he is inheriting is reduced by 90% to give the agricultural value, which in this example results in a figure of €400,000. As he does not exceed his threshold for 2008 (€521,208), he pays no tax.

What if Sean failed the farmer test because the value of his own house, which is in his sole name and is a non-agricultural asset, is €1,000,000? Well, if he is married then there is a little scope for some post death tax planning.

Between the date of his father's death and the date the Grant of Probate issues, which could be six months or more, Sean can legitimately transfer his house to his wife, which means he will only be assessed on the bank account when the figures are calculated, i.e., his house worth €1,000,000 is ignored as it is now in his wife's name.

Therefore his total assets at the valuation date are €4,004,000 of which €4,000,000 is agricultural in nature, giving a percentage of 99.90%, meaning that he would once again pass the farmer test and can avail of the relief.

Gift or inheritance of money invested in agricultural property
If you receive cash by way of gift or inheritance with a specific instruction that you invest it in agricultural property and you proceed to invest the money in agricultural property within the strict two year time limit, then you can probably avail of agricultural relief. Remember, you must still pass the 80% test. So, much would depend on the value of your own assets. If you do not invest within two years you cannot claim the relief and tax must be paid.

Business Relief
Business relief was introduced by the Finance Act 1994. It applies to both gifts and inheritances.

The idea of the relief is to prevent as far as possible, the sale or break up of businesses, especially family businesses, due to tax liabilities and to encourage and reward enterprise. So, if you inherited a business and then faced a massive tax bill as a result, you may have no choice

but to sell the business or a part of the business to pay the tax. Therefore, tax plays an important role in the transfer of a business from one generation to the next.

Business relief is similar to Agricultural relief, and so the saving is also 90%. The relief applies to 'relevant business property'. This means the disponer must have a business or an interest in a business and it applies to both a sole trader and a partnership.

Certain businesses which consist wholly or mainly of dealings in currencies, securities, stocks or shares, land or buildings, making or holding investments, are however excluded and will not qualify for the relief. The word 'Business' should include any business that is carried on for making a profit or gain. It would of course cover professions such as accountants and architects, and trades such as publicans and carpenters.

Individual assets used in a business such as a factory or building will not qualify for the relief unless they are transferred to the beneficiary along with the business.

There is a minimum period of ownership. To qualify, the relevant business property must have been part of the business on a continuous basis prior to the date of the gift or inheritance for two years in the case of an inheritance and five years in any other case, e.g. a gift, or an inheritance taken on the death of a life tenant.

The relief is applied to the taxable value of the business. This is slightly different to agricultural relief, which applies to the market value of agricultural property.

Example:
Stephen left his entire estate by will to his son Mark.
The estate contains a delivery business worth €1,400,000, a house worth €300,000, a

personal bank account with €25,000, and a business account of €40,000.

There are business liabilities amounting to €175,000, trade debts of €22,000, funeral costs of €4,000, and legal costs of €15,000.

GROSS NON-BUSINESS PROPERTY			GROSS BUSINESS PROPERTY		
Personal bank account		€25,000	Delivery Business		€1,400,000
House		€300,000	Bank		€40,000
Total		€325,000	Total		€1,440,000
Less:			Less:		
Costs	€15,000		Liabilities	€175,000	
Funeral	€4,000	€19,000	Trade Debts	€22,000	€197,000
Taxable value		€306,000	Value		€1,243,000
			Business relief (90%)		€1,118,700
			Taxable value		€124,300

The taxable value of all assets is €430,300 (€306,000 + €124,300). Mark is below his Group A threshold of €521,208 and so pays no tax.

What's the difference between agricultural relief and business relief?
There is no minimum period of ownership for agricultural relief – either two or five years are required for business relief.

A gift or inheritance of money can be used to purchase agricultural assets and so in certain cases can qualify for agricultural relief. But there is no similar facility available for business relief.

If you fail to qualify for agricultural relief you can still apply for business relief as a farm is technically a business. But you cannot choose which relief to claim. If the benefit is agricultural, you must apply for agricultural relief first and if you fail then you can try business relief. But this does not operate in reverse. If you fail business relief you cannot try to claim agricultural relief.

Favourite Niece / Nephew Relief
Favourite nephew or niece relief doesn't mean that a person has a 'favourite' niece or nephew. It means a niece or nephew who is receiving a gift or inheritance of a business and who has worked in the business with an aunt or uncle and who is claiming the relief.

Here's how it works:
The relief applies to a niece or a nephew who has worked substantially on a full time basis for the disponer for the period of five years ending on the date the disponer gives the business to the niece or nephew, or dies. The niece or nephew must have worked at least 15 hours a week in a small business (where there is only the disponer, his spouse and the niece/nephew) or 24 hours a week in a large business (where there are other employees).

Note that farming is a business and so a farm can qualify for the relief. The niece/nephew must be a blood relation so nieces/nephews by marriage won't qualify.

Once the niece/nephew qualifies they move from a group B threshold into a group A threshold. The relief only applies to a business and business property. If there is an inheritance of both business and non-business assets then the group A threshold will apply to the business assets and the group B threshold will apply to the non-business assets.

This relief can be claimed at the same time as agricultural or business relief. Qualifying as a favourite niece or nephew moves you up to a higher threshold while agricultural or business relief drives down the value of the land or the business itself. If you qualify for both you may completely eliminate any tax liability.

DWELLINGHOUSE RELIEF
Dwellinghouse relief applies to a gift or inheritance of a house in which the beneficiary is currently residing. The parties don't have to be related so anyone can claim this relief.

How do you get the relief?
1. **Inheritance** – you receive the house when someone dies.
You,(the beneficiary) must have occupied the dwellinghouse as your only or main residence

for a period of three years prior to the disponer's death. You must not be beneficially entitled to any other house or an interest in any other house. You must continue to occupy the house as your only or main residence for six years from the date of the inheritance otherwise the relief will be clawed back. This last condition however does not apply if you are 55 or over or if you die within the six years.

2. Gift – you receive the house from a living person.
For a gift the requirements were changed by the Finance Act 2007 and are relevant from the 20th February 2007. These conditions are more onerous on the beneficiary. As for an inheritance above, you must have occupied the dwellinghouse as your only or main residence for a period of three years prior to the date of the gift.

However, and this is important, the beneficiary must have been compelled to occupy the house by reason of the disponer's old age or infirmity and the disponer must depend on the services of the beneficiary for that period. You must not be entitled to any other house or an interest in any other house. The disponer must own the house for those three years prior to transferring it to you. You (the beneficiary) must continue to reside in the house for six years from the date of the gift, otherwise the relief will be clawed back. Again, the conditions don't apply if the beneficiary is 55 or over or dies within the six years.

In both cases the relief will not be withdrawn (clawed back) where the house is sold because you require long term medical care in a hospital or nursing home. You don't have to be related to the person giving you the house. If you qualify for the relief, it provides a total exemption from tax. Better still, your threshold will remain intact.

Heritage Property
Full relief is available for heritage objects and property in the State. Examples would be pictures, prints, books, manuscripts, works of art, jewellery, scientific collections etc which the Revenue deem to be items of national, scientific, historic or artistic interest.

To get the relief, you must keep the object in the State unless the absence of the item is approved by the Revenue Commissioners. You must allow members of the public reasonable access to view it and the object must not be held for trading purposes.

Other Exemptions and Reliefs from CAT
There are numerous other reliefs and exemptions available but the more common ones are mentioned here:

1. Qualifying expenses of incapacitated people.
   Where a beneficiary receives money exclusively for the purpose of discharging qualifying expenses of a person permanently incapacitated by reason of physical or mental infirmity, that benefit is exempt from CAT provided the Revenue

Commissioners are satisfied that the money was or will be applied for such a purpose. "Qualifying expenses" are expenses relating to medical care including the cost of maintenance in connection with such medical care.

2. Money received by a person by way of compensation for suffering an injury is exempt.

3. Winnings from legal betting or the lottery are also exempt.

4. Gifts to recognised charities are exempt. Gifts from charities are also exempt. (An example would be a gift of a scholarship from an educational trust).

5. If a parent gave a child a gift of a house within the last five years and the parent is now receiving it back on the death of the child, the inheritance will be entirely exempt.

CLAWBACK (WITHDRAWAL OF TAX RELIEF)

Where any relief from tax has been obtained and the beneficiary subsequently disposes of the asset or it is compulsorily acquired (by a local authority) within the 'clawback' period, or doesn't comply with some aspect of the granting of the relief, then the original tax relief may be subject to re-adjustment by the Revenue and may result in tax that was originally avoided because you obtained the relief having to be paid.

For example, if you sell the asset on which you obtained relief, then the value of the asset will be re-adjusted for tax purposes. The purpose of 'clawback' is to prevent people from obtaining tax relief and then selling the asset to make a profit. It is an anti-avoidance measure.

There are different clawback periods for different reliefs but the main ones are as follows:

1. Agricultural Relief

If for example, you inherited a farm and got agricultural relief. If you sell all or part of the farm within six years or it is compulsorily acquired by a local authority, and you do not replace the farm with other farm property within one year of the sale or six years of the CPO (Compulsory Purchase Order), then you may lose the relief and tax will have to be paid. The six year period is extended to ten years where land is sold for development purposes. There is no clawback if you die before the property is sold or compulsorily acquired.

2. Business Relief

If the business ceases trading within six years of the date of the gift or inheritance and is not replaced by another business within one year, then the relief is clawed back. Or, if the business is sold or compulsorily acquired within the six year period and is not replaced by other relevant business property within one year. Similar to agricultural relief, business relief will not be clawed back if the beneficiary dies before the business is sold or compulsorily acquired.

3. Dwellinghouse

Relief will be withdrawn where the beneficiary does not continue to occupy the house for six years after they receive it. However, if the beneficiary dies within the six years the relief will not be clawed back.

OTHER TAXES AND DUTIES

Trust Tax

Trusts are usually set up to provide for children under 18 or perhaps for a child or young adult suffering from a severe mental or physical disability. In order to avail of certain tax reliefs, a separate trust with separate property / assets should be set up specifically for a disabled child.

CAT is payable where the beneficiary exceeds their threshold.

However, where a discretionary trust is set up trust tax can also arise. The tax is payable at (six per cent) 6% and this is a once-off payment. It can be reduced to 3% if the trust is fully wound up within five years. There is also an annual tax payable of 1% over the life of the trust.

With careful planning, a discretionary trust is very useful both from a legal and a tax perspective. It can be complex and you should consult an accountant or tax adviser before setting up a discretionary trust.

Capital Gains Tax (CGT)

What is CGT?
CGT is a tax that arises on the sale or disposal of an asset. Basically it is the 'gain' that is subject to the tax. So, if you acquired an asset for example shares in a company, for €50,000 in 2006 and sold them for €60,000 in 2008, then you have made a gain of €10,000 and must pay tax on that gain at 20%.

What is the difference between a sale and a disposal?
If you sell an asset, you get money for it. That's straightforward. A disposal however, though it can include a sale, usually means that an asset (or part of an asset) is transferred from one person to another but the recipient doesn't pay for it, i.e. no money changes hands.

This is a voluntary transfer. So here, because you don't have a sale and therefore, no payment, the Revenue will require a valuation of the property being disposed of and the tax will be charged on the value of the asset. This is an anti-avoidance measure to prevent the disposal of assets for less than their value, i.e. to avoid paying tax.

Penalties for undervaluation can be charged at up to 5% or 10% of the value of the gain depending on the level of undervaluation. Interest is charged for overdue payments and is currently 0.0273% per day. So do not even think of hoodwinking the taxman by understating the value.

CGT does not arise when someone dies. However, assets acquired by inheritance or gift are deemed to be acquired at market value at the date of the gift or death and the first charge to CGT will arise on a subsequent sale or disposal.

How much is the tax?
Capital Gains Tax is currently 20%.

When is the tax payable?
On a sale or disposal between 1 January and 30 September in any year the tax is due on or before 31 October of that year. or disposal made between 1 October and 31 December in any year, the tax is due on or before 31 January of the following year.

Exemptions, reliefs and deductions from CGT
The first €1,270 of any gain made is free of tax. There is no CGT on a transfer of a site to a child for the purpose of that child constructing a house. The size of the site is limited to 0.407 hectares (or one acre) and the value of the site cannot exceed €500,000.

When dealing with the CGT on the transfer of a site to a child, the exemption of €500,000 with regard to the value of the site exists, but also a parent can claim the Retirement Relief up to €750,000 and marginal relief in excess of €750,000, in the event of the site being greater than one acre or the value in excess of €500,000.

If you are over 55 and have owned and farmed land for 10 years or more, you can avail of relief up to €750,000.

A transfer to a young trained farmer is exempt from CGT. Disposals to spouses (and assets being split between divorcing spouses) are exempt. Similar recognition will be extended to qualifying cohabiting and gay couples once the bills in these areas become law.

There is no CGT payable on the sale of your principal private residence as long as the grounds with the house do not exceed one acre.

Spouses

Under the CGT rules in respect of private residences, if you build a house, live in it for a period of time and then move on, the Revenue could well treat this as property development rather than a private venture and so it may be subject to CGT.

STAMP DUTY

When does a charge to Stamp Duty arise?

Stamp duty is payable on a wide range of legal and commercial documents, including (but not limited to) conveyances, transfers and leases of property, share transfers and certain agreements. When you pay the duty the Revenue put a stamp on the document showing the value of the duty paid. The duty is usually paid by the purchaser or beneficiary.

Even where no money changes hands between the seller and buyer, stamp duty can arise on the 'market value' of the asset. These are called voluntary transfers and usually arise where a person is giving a gift of property.

Here, the Revenue Commissioners will seek a valuation of the property being transferred. This is the market value of the property i.e. the price the house would achieve if sold on the open market. The stamp duty is then based on that value even though no money is changing hands.

Rate of Duty for Non-Residential Property

UP TO	€10,000		EXEMPT	
	€10,001	to	€20,000	1%
	€20,001	to	€30,000	2%
	€30,001	to	€40,000	3%
	€40,001	to	€70,000	4%
	€70,001	to	€80,000	5%
	€80,001	to	€100,000	6%
	€100,001	to	€120,000	7%
	€120,001	to	€150,000	8%
	OVER	€150,000	9%	

For a residential property the stamp duty is payable as follows:

First	€125,000	exempt
Next	€875,000	7%
Balance		9%

For a sale or transfer of shares in a company the stamp duty is payable at 1% of the value. Sometimes, rather than just purchasing land from a company and paying a huge amount of stamp duty, you may consider buying the company itself and just paying 1%.

Stamp duty can apply to an inheritance too. In the case of a deed of family arrangement, which is essentially an agreement drawn up by the various beneficiaries in an estate, where they fundamentally alter the terms of a will, this can be subject to stamp duty.

Guidenote: You don't actually alter the will itself. The Deed of Family Arrangement makes an adjustment to benefits received only if the family all agree after a person has died.

EXEMPTIONS AND RELIEFS FROM STAMP DUTY

EXEMPTIONS
Spouses
Transfers between spouses in many cases won't attract stamp duty. There is a complete exemption from stamp duty where the family home is being transferred from one spouse to another or into their joint names. Also, property transferred between separating or divorcing spouses as part of the separation or divorce is exempt from stamp duty.

Inter Company Transfers
Inter company transfers are exempt from duty where the companies are 90% related or associated.

Transfer to Young Trained Farmer
If a farmer wants to retire or set a child up in farming then this can be done without paying stamp duty. As long as the beneficiary holds one of the required certificates of education from the list of approved bodies (Teagasc etc) and he or she is under 35, then full relief is available.

Approved sports bodies and charities are also exempt provided certain conditions are met.

RELIEFS
First time buyer and owner/occupier relief are not covered here as they don't really arise in an inheritance or succession situation. However we should inform you that if you take an inheritance and later you are a first time buyer of a property, you still get your first time buyer relief.

Transfer of a Site from Parent to a Child
There is no stamp duty on a transfer of a site to a child for the purpose of that child constructing their principal private residence. The size of the site is limited to .407 hectares (or one acre) and the value of the site cannot exceed €500,000. 'Child' can include a foster child where they meet certain conditions.

Consanguinity (blood) Relief
Where the parties to a sale (or transfer) and purchase of property are related or associated

then the purchaser / transferee can claim consanguinity relief. The stamp duty that would normally be paid is reduced by half.

Farm Consolidation Relief
Relief is available where a farmer sells land and purchases land in order to consolidate his/her holding. The relief is also available for exchanges of land.

On all taxes, penalties and interest are a major issue and a situation could arise where a person fails to make a return or believes that he / she does not have to make one and has a subsequent audit. Whilst he / she would owe no tax, he / she would still get caught for penalties for failing to make the correct return on time.

Clawback of Stamp Duty
If you obtain stamp duty relief then the Revenue usually require that you hold on to the land or property for a minimum period of time, usually three years. If you decided to sell or dispose of the property or even a site within that time, then the relief may be clawed back and stamp duty will have to be paid. If you sell or dispose after the time has expired the relief will not be clawed back.

FOREIGN ASSETS AND DOUBLE TAXATION
Where you have immovable property in a foreign country but you reside in Ireland, after your death, your estate / beneficiary may have to pay two taxes, one in Ireland by virtue of your residence / domicile and one in the foreign country where the asset is located. This is called 'double taxation' and it can cause hardship in certain cases.

The Revenue have allowed for certain types of relief from double taxation. These reliefs are quite complex and beyond the scope of this book but they must be mentioned to make you aware as many people now with foreign assets may not have obtained the appropriate tax advice when they purchased their foreign property.

CGT, just like CAT, can arise on a foreign asset. If you sell or dispose of for example a house or apartment abroad, it may be subject to CGT both in Ireland by virtue of your domicile / residence, and abroad by virtue of the location of the property. You may of course be able to avail of double taxation arrangements which can provide some relief from the taxes arising.

Bilateral Relief and Unilateral Relief
There are bilateral agreements between Ireland and other countries, namely the UK and the USA. Unilateral relief is granted only where there is no double taxation treaty in force.

UK
Under the UK convention the country where the property is not situated gives a credit for

tax paid in the country where the property is situated. Credit is only given when the same property is taxed in both countries on the same event.

USA

As the USA claims to tax assets wherever situated if the deceased is a US citizen at the time of death, irrespective of the domicile, it often results in both Ireland and the US claiming tax on worldwide assets.

Under the convention, if the deceased died domiciled and resident in Ireland but was a citizen of the US at the date of death, Ireland will allow a credit for the US tax payable on that property. The credit given is the lesser of the Irish or US tax on the property. The US on the other hand will allow against its tax on property situated in Ireland a credit again equal to the lesser of the Ireland or US taxes.

See information on double taxation in the IT39 Revenue guide.

COHABITANTS AND SAME SEX COUPLES

According to the Census of 2006, co-habitants make up 11.6% of all family units and there are over 2000 gay couples residing together. A third of all births in Ireland are outside marriage to either lone parents or cohabiting couples.

In Ireland, just like most other EU countries, co-habitation is on the increase as are marital breakdown and divorce. Cohabitants usually comprise young couples living together before they marry, people in long term relationships who feel indifferent about marriage and older people who may have been married before and who are now in a new relationship but do not wish to re-marry.

Where a man and woman live together but are not married they sometimes refer to themselves as 'common law spouses' and they may think they have similar legal, tax and social welfare rights, to married couples. However, the term 'common law spouse' has no legal meaning whatsoever, so the reality is, they have no legal rights in this area. Cohabiting gay couples are in a similar situation and they too are not afforded the rights of married couples.

The government, following a report by the Law Reform Commission in 2006, are currently reviewing the issues. It's doubtful they will introduce civil marriage for gay couples due to potential problems with the Constitution. That issue may be left over for another day, but urgent reform of the law is required for same sex and opposite sex co-habiting couples to give them equal status to that of spouses in the areas of property, pensions, social welfare, family law and succession matters and tax. It is unlikely that the law relating to cohabitants in non-sexual relationships, such as brothers, sisters and other family members, will be changed.

The issues need to be addressed in an effort to provide fairness, security and equality for all.

CONCLUSION

This book is intended to be a general guide only to the various taxes, duties, exemptions and reliefs that will arise in an inheritance or succession situation. Tax laws, bands and thresholds are changed and updated almost annually by the Government's Finance Acts. Generally the taxes and duties that affect us most will be covered by the national and local newspapers, TV and so on.

If you have a general query look at the revenue website on www.revenue.ie or the government's citizens' information website provided by Comhairle, www.citizensinformation.ie. Both websites are easy to navigate and are user friendly.

If your problem is more specific or technical you should consult your accountant, tax adviser or solicitor. You will no doubt be charged a fee for the advice but it could result in huge savings and be money well spent for the long run.

SUCCESSION

In life you should make the most of it whether your desire is to have fun, create happiness for others or just grow rich. Whether you are a parent, a grandparent of 100 plus or a young adult aged just over the age of 18, succession planning will give you direction on how to get most from your career and your life.

Good succession planning may help you to gain financial independence, grow your business, help you provide for children, avail of tax incentives, provide for illness, help you retire early and create harmony in your home.

This planning may give direction to you, your spouse / partner and your children, and extended family. It may avoid stress and uncertainty for children, family and friends for years to come.

Deciding *Succession*

The earth is not ours to keep. It is a treasure we merely hold in trust for future generations.

- Anon

In a perfect world, succession planning is a gradual and phased transfer of your estate to your spouse, partner, child, children, or business partner over a lifetime or several lifetimes.

Your estate may be your home, business, farm, assets such as money in the bank, and investments whether in property, bonds, commodities, equities.

Your ideal succession plan provides for your security, and reward for the chosen members of the succession partnership. It provides for care, independence and dignity of parents in senior times.

Optimum Time Opportunities

The plan will transfer your estate at the best or optimum time or times to your successor ('heir', 'heiress', 'partner' or 'next generation') over your lifetime so that you can avail of lifetime opportunities, tax, investments and so on.

Succession planning will apply mainly if you have a house, investment property, business, or farm and if you have a family.
In anticipation of your senior times, you may consider that it is worth your while gradually transfering ownership and management of your home or business over a son or daughter, niece, nephew or in-law. This may involve co-operation in building an extension to your home or modifying access and facilities or building or renting a new home and organising finance to do so.

For a profitable business entity, the advantage of planned succession may be that your spouse, partner, son or daughter is interested in the business and knowledgeable about it. It may benefit everybody to arrange a partnership so that you now will have greater security for yourself and your husband / wife / partner and son or daughter will have a more secure future too.

Two people instead of one will be interested in developing the business. You may save on tax and gain on other incentives. The business may be transferred to the son or daughter over a period of time. Agreements may be designed to suit the special and particular circumstances of each individual. It may have inbuilt 'warming up', 'cooling off' and 'opt out' clauses as many partnerships do not work out.

Approaches to Succession Planning

The first thing to be considered as part of any succession plan is a will. You will get advice from a solicitor on tax thresholds, and the law, not to mention information on how and when to time transfers and gifts to chosen beneficiaries.

Joint Ownership

An asset will usually be put into joint names where two (or more) people acquiring it have done so by contributing equally or unequally to the purchase price.

This is very important when planning succession and inheritance. For the purpose of explanation, we will only assume ownership of property by two people. By 'property' we mean houses, land, shares, and so on.

There are two ways in which people can hold property jointly. One is as 'joint tenants'. The other is as 'tenants in common'.

'Joint tenants' means two or more people own an equal share in the asset and they each have the right to use the asset. If they want to mortgage it or sell it then they must both agree on the mortgage or sale. There is no physical division of the property but each owner is equally entitled to all of the property. In the event of the death of one of the joint tenants, the other will take the entire property automatically.

'Tenants in common' is similar but there are a number of key differences. The first is that the ownership doesn't have to be equal. One person can own 75% and the other 25%. The second is that when one of the owners dies, the other doesn't take the entire property automatically but instead it will pass in accordance with the deceased's will or on intestacy rules. (See chart in Making a Will.)

Effectively, this can result in many people becoming owners of the one property.

Another point worth noting is, where people hold property as tenants in common, they can each raise a mortgage on their specific share of the property. More importantly, they can leave it by will to someone else. As we can see, 'Joint tenants' and 'Tenants in common' have very different meanings and as a result they can have very different consequences when it comes to considering your succession plan and your will.

There are other assets of course that can be held jointly and typically these would include bank or building society accounts, credit union accounts, post office accounts and even prize bonds. These will be given separate treatment below.

1. Jointly owned houses and land

Jointly owned houses and land is best illustrated by three examples:

(i) A married couple buy a house

Paul and Sinead are both in their thirties and have been going out for years. They just got married and have decided to buy their own place. They work out their finances, organise the mortgage and go in to see their solicitor. As they are both working, and both contributing equally to the purchase price, they would like the house to be in both of their names.

In this situation the solicitor will typically suggest that the house be put in their joint names as joint tenants. This means that if one of them dies, the survivor will get the property automatically. Even if Paul had made a will leaving everything to his mother, his wife will still get the house as joint property passes outside the will.

In other words the reason the solicitor suggested placing the property in their names as 'joint tenants' was to benefit (his wife) on his death.

This is called 'survivorship' and is usually found in a husband and wife situation. It is always open to Paul and Sinead to hold the house as tenants in common, but this is a little less common.

(ii). An unmarried couple buy a house

Joanne and Barry are both 21 and have been going out for a year and are not married. Joanne is expecting a baby so they decide to buy a house together. They provide the funds equally.

There is always a risk, as with any relationship, when a couple buy a house together that their relationship may not last. The solicitor may suggest that where property is held as tenants in common, that they put in place a 'co-ownership agreement'. This is an agreement that states what is to happen to the property in the event that the couple split up. The house is therefore placed in their joint names as tenants in common.

The ownership of the house is still equal. However if Barry dies, Joanne will not get the entire

house. Instead, Barry's share of the house will pass either in accordance with the terms of his will or it will pass on intestacy where there is no will.

Of course he may well leave it by will to Joanne but if he didn't make a will then Barry's parent(s) will inherit his share of the property (as their child is not yet born) with the result that his parents and Joanne will become the owners of the property as tenants in common. They can if they wish insist at the time of buying the house that they are joint owners as joint tenants, meaning that the survivor will inherit.

(iii) Two brothers buy a House
John and Brendan are brothers and they want to buy a house to get out from under their mother's feet. John is 28 and Brendan is 22.

As John is earning more than Brendan, he provides 75% of the purchase money with Brendan providing 25%.

In this example they would have to hold the property as tenants in common in unequal shares. In the event of a sale then no doubt, John in particular would want to get his 75% of the sale proceeds. Here, each person holds a distinct share in the property to the value of the funds they provide but remember that each still has the right to the use of the entire property.

Effect on Wills
Property held under a joint tenancy passes by what is known as 'survivorship' which basically means that the person who lives longest gets the property. Even if there are 10 owners, the last man or woman standing will get the property. So such property won't be affected by the provisions of your will.

Sometimes people will put all of their property in joint names in an effort to save the survivor having to go through the hassle of Probate. This can be a useful way to hold property as it automatically provides for the survivor in the event of death. Remember, even if you receive property by survivorship, tax can arise as you are receiving a half share of something for nothing.

Joint bank Accounts
Bank accounts can be different. More often than not if two people are living together either

as a married couple or as cohabitants, then they may well have a joint bank account. A joint bank account can be handy for paying household bills, mortgage and so on. Typically, both people will lodge equal amounts of money into the account. This is a true joint account.

Some accounts are opened in joint names from the start. Sometimes an account is opened in one person's name and another person is added at a later stage. This may not be a true joint account. Much can depend on the relationship that the two people have e.g., husband and wife, father and son, partners / cohabitants. More importantly a lot will depend on who provided the money in the account.

If it was provided jointly by the parties to the account then obviously this is a joint account in every sense. But what if all the money is provided by just one of the parties to the account?

Prior to 1996 the courts refused to recognise that a joint bank account gave rise to succession rights based on survivorship where only one party provided the money. They were viewed as what is known as a 'resulting trust' which means that the money in the account was to be held by the survivor but they didn't get to keep it. Instead they were deemed to hold it on trust for the benefit of the deceased person's estate.

The exception to this was where the survivor was the wife or child of the person who provided the money. Where the couple are married it doesn't matter who provides the money as there is a presumption that the survivor gets it. In any other case, e.g. where the money is provided in unequal shares, and / or where the parties aren't married, then the presumption is that the survivor won't get the money in the account.

Remember, much will depend on the instructions given to the bank when the account is opened. Even if the parties to the account are not married or if the money isn't provided equally, if the account is set up with an instruction to benefit the survivor then the money in the account will pass to the survivor. Don't leave it to chance. Be clear to as to what you want to happen to the account when you die.

Credit Union

Credit Union accounts are very popular. When you open your credit union account you will be asked by the cashier if you would like to nominate the proceeds of the account to someone (known as a nominee) after your death. Almost everyone completes the nomination form and once completed it will be kept with your account details and noted on the computer system at the credit union office.

When you die, the nomination becomes relevant. If for example you made a will leaving all your property to your sister but your credit union account is nominated to your brother, then your sister will get everything except the credit union account. This is because nominated property is not caught by the terms of your will. In other words, the nominated account is deemed to pass to your brother the minute you die and it will not form part of your estate.

Obviously if this is what was desired then that's ok. But what if the credit union account was your only asset and you really wanted your sister to have it? In that case as your estate contains no assets, there is no point in administering it. The one wish you had will not be fulfilled as your brother and not your sister will get the account.

This is clearly not ideal and indeed it can cause problems, especially if the brother and sister don't get on. He would most likely have no intention of disclaiming his interest in the account for the benefit of his sister.

Life Insurance / Assurance Policies
When you take out an insurance or assurance policy you will be asked by the broker or agent to nominate a person whom you would like to receive the proceeds of the policy after your death. Sometimes insurance companies will refer to the nominee as the beneficiary, which is the same title given to someone who is receiving a gift or inheritance. The title is not relevant as it means the same thing.

If you nominate your husband to be the nominee/beneficiary of the policy after your death then he is entitled to the proceeds of the policy as soon as you die. He may not actually receive the proceeds of the policy until the claim has been approved. As the policy does not form part of the estate he does not have to wait until the Grant of Probate comes out.

The fact that the policy is nominated means that it passes on the death of the nominator/donor to the nominee/beneficiary usually on production of the death certificate and completing a claim form.

Effect on Wills
When you are making a will, consider carefully property that you may have already nominated to another person. It can make a huge difference to the value of your estate as such property may not have been included in the reckoning. Policies and accounts that you thought would pass under the terms of your will may actually pass to someone else.

In many cases the nominee may be the person to whom you have left everything under your will. If so there will be no problems. The potential for problems arises where the nominee or beneficiary of the account or policy is not the intended recipient. This usually happens when the account or policy was taken out some years ago and through the passage of time you may simply have forgotten that the account was nominated to someone else.

Even if you don't have a will made, nominated property and accounts still pass to the nominee or beneficiary you have named, as such accounts and policies fall outside your estate.

However, the beneficiary may have a tax liability as the benifit is still an inheritance.

SUCCESSION PLANS
House as Main Asset
Pat and Mary moved back from England in the 1960s. They bought a site and built a house. Their family is reared and they have now retired. They have three adult children none of whom is dependant on them. Each of the children is doing fine and Pat and Mary don't see any reason to favour one over any of the others.

Having discussed this with their solicitor they appointed their oldest child as executor for convenience of administration of the estate and they directed the executor to sell the house after their death and to divide the proceeds equally among the three children. They have a little bit of money in the bank and some small savings policies. This they call the 'residue' and they make provision in their will that the residue is also to be divided equally among the three children.

Q.   What happens if one of the children falls on hard times?
A.   Pat and Mary can change their wills.

Q.   Should Pat and Mary not have arranged to transfer their house/home into the names of the three children now to save them the trouble of administering the estate?
A.   Certainly not. Pat and Mary need to retain their own independence and security. If they become ill they might have to sell the house themselves and use the proceeds to pay for medical and nursing home care.

Business Plan
Darren and Catherine married in 1985. They were both busy with their careers but following the arrival of two children they decided that Catherine would concentrate on her interests on her internet business and Darren would take on only a little consultancy work as it suited him.

Their main asset was their house which they had purchased in joint names. They bought a property in Spain. Fortunately they consulted a good professional who advised them to put a will in place in Spain to deal with the Spanish property only. This avoids difficulties where the Spanish authorities may refuse to recognise an Irish will when dealing with Spanish property.

They also took advice in relation to an Irish will and were careful about the wording of the Irish will so that it affected their Irish and other property only and not the Spanish property.

When the children were young Darren and Catherine decided to make wills whereby each left everything to the other but in the event of them dying together (or within a short time of each other following, or example a car crash or plane crash) they appointed trustees to hold onto and deal with all property for the benefit of their children until the youngest child reaches 18. At that stage, the trustees have power to decide which child gets what. This seems like a very onerous discretionary power for the trustees.

The point however is that if Darren or Catherine survived they obviously would have full discretion as to what they would wish to do with the property having regard to the position of the children at that stage. It seems sensible therefore that if they are picking two good trustees, they should leave the trustees with the same type of discretion rather than locking the trustees into a situation where they would have to treat all children equally in relation to the assets. For various good reasons most parents do not treat all children equally when it comes to division of assets.

Darren and Catherine had further discussions about Catherine's business and in one of their review meetings with the accountant it became clear that Catherine's business was becoming quite valuable. Darren had no specific interest in the business as such and, conscious of the fact that he would inherit it completely if Catherine died suddenly, he wondered if some of the shares in the business (Catherine had formed a company) should be transferred to the children, particularly the oldest child who was showing a considerable aptitude for computers / internet related matters.

It was decided to transfer a 25% shareholding in the company to the child as the company seemed destined to become even more valuable. Even with business relief it is possible that a future transfer to the child would be possible. The important thing here is to strike a balance between the owner remaining flexible in the event of a sale of the business and tax considerations with regard to transfer of the business to children. Note that the transfer of shares was only done when the 'child' was 18. Otherwise there could have been a difficulty in the event that a buyer came along at a good price for the company. Catherine would not have been able to sell because the child being under 18 would not have been able to sign a valid contract.

On receiving the shares, the child became actively involved in the running of the company with Catherine. Over time, it became clear to Darren and Catherine that their other child was not going to take an interest in the company. Having regard to issues of company control it was decided not to advance any share holding to the other child. Darren and Catherine were anxious to release some cash from the business and so they arranged that their child who worked in the business with them would raise a loan and pay them for a further tranche or slice of shareholding thus giving them capital which they could spend and also enabling them to make a substantial payment to their other child towards the purchase of a separate business or property.

Darren and Catherine revised their wills so that on the death of the survivor the remaining

shareholding in the company would be left to their child working in the business, subject to a payment of perhaps 10% of the value of the business to the other child.

If they didn't want to burden the child recieving the business with debt, then an alternative would be to leave the Spanish property to the other child. This all of course depends on Darren's and Catherine's appraisal of the situation in life of their children. If for instance they were satisfied that their children were doing well enough without any further property then they could decide to make a sizeable bequest to charity.

In their mid 50s, both Darren and Catherine had to deal with a parent suffering from Alzheimer's disease. They are conscious therefore of difficulties which can arise when somebody is unable to make a decision on their own affairs and so Darren and Catherine attended their solicitor and each put in place an enduring power of attorney document to deal with their personal care of decisions and business affairs in the event that they lose the mental capacity to do so themselves.

Farm Succession Plan

The young farmer at home has been to agricultural college and is a hard worker. There is an argument. He/she has a full blown row with 'the Boss' over an aspect of farm management, an aspect which is not absolutely crucial to the running of the farm.

The row however is enough to stop people talking to each other for a week. Everybody feels hurt. Communication is strained. There is misunderstanding. Productivity begins to slip. Without discussion, attitudes become entrenched and relationships sour. What do you do?

Without a doubt all that is needed to get things back on track is discussion. Get talking about it to someone. Try to choose someone who is respected by both the older and the younger farmer. It needn't be a big professional consultation on a formal fee paying basis. It could be a favourite aunt, an uncle or a trusted neighbour.

If you need to go to a professional you must be prepared to pay for it although in many cases the solicitor or accountant won't charge a fee. If the difficulty concerns farm management, talk to an experienced farm management consultant or your Teagasc advisor.

Realise that there is no plan or expert on earth who will show you how to run a farm or business at 100% efficiency 100% of the time. Does it really matter if the young farmer has a slightly different method, provided the job gets done? These issues must be worked out, discussed fully and be running smoothly before a transfer of all or part of the farm is even considered.

Transfer Time

As parents get older they are likely to go and see their solicitor and discuss the possibility of transferring all or part of the business or farm to their son/daughter who is actually farming the land or running the business. Sometimes there will still be younger children at home being put through their education. As a holding measure, the parents might first just make a will.

In many cases there is no farmer at home or the farmer is only part time and his main work is off-farm. While the fact of having no successor working on the farm is tinged with sadness, it actually makes the succession plan easier. As no child is dependant on the farm the parents will often direct that after their deaths the farm is to be sold and the sale proceeds divided equally among the children. None of them actually need it or more likely want it as a farming enterprise.

It gets a little more complicated if there is a part-time farmer who has an obvious love of the land but simply must concentrate on off farm work to make ends meet. In this situation farming parents frequently don't want to take the farm away from the young farmer. They will often leave him the farm but will oblige him to make certain payments to other family members.

Example: Jim and Margaret own 80 acres. They have reared four children. The three oldest children live in different parts of the country. They are all doing reasonably well. The youngest child has built his own house on a site across the road from the 'home place'. He works hard five days a week as a steel erector and gets his farming done either early in the morning or late in the evening and on Saturdays and Sundays with some assistance from his parents who are both retired and in receipt of a contributory old age pension. The holding at today's prices is probably worth at least 1.5 million euro.

Jim and Margaret have taken advice on the site potential and have been advised that they should receive planning permission for two sites if required. They don't want to sell sites themselves but armed with that knowledge and the fact that sites in the area are being sold for €100,000 each they feel it would be easy enough on a commercial basis to make the son's inheritance subject to a payment of €100,000 each to the other three children.

Q. Should the parents consider a transfer now of this farm in addition to the will?

A. Probably not as the son is not wholly dependant on the farm. Why should the parents divest themselves of their main asset/security? There is also the problem that because the son is mostly engaged in off-farm work he would not get stamp duty exemption and so on a transfer of a Euro 1.5 million farm he would pay stamp duty of 4.5%. A large waste of money.

The Partnerships Option

Father and son. Father and mother and son and daughter in law. Mother and daughter and son-in law. Business colleague and business colleague. Farmer and neighbouring farmer. The options for the formation of partnerships are many. If you are considering the formation of a partnership as a means of planning your succession think it through carefully.

A partnership is an agreement between two or more people who are in business together or who wish to get into business together.

The partnership requires that the partners describe how they are going to manage and run the business together as a unit, what the assets and liabilities are, and how profit is to be shared.

When thinking of the subjects of inheritance and succession, the business partners if they are parent and child should think of how the business is to be gradually transferred from one to another.

Partnerships have pros and cons. A major part of the success of a partnership requires good communication between all parties and great amounts of tolerance and endurance for the long term. Partnerships should be considered as part of the succession process and in particular where there is a family business or a family farm situation.

The guidebook *Farm Family Partnerships*, editor Jim Cleary, published 27 years ago by Macra na Feirme and the Incorporated Law Society of Ireland contains advice that is relevant today to both ordinary business and farming business. It says that a farm family partnership has many advantages, the chief ones being:

- Greater security for both partners
- Parent can involve the child without giving everything away
- Parent and child have the status of farm partners instead of employer / employee
- Two people interested in developing the farm, instead of one
- Savings - e.g. Income Tax
- Farm can be transferred over period of time
- Elevates the child and gives a feeling of achievement

In a family farm situation, a partnership arrangement gives greater long term security to the son and therefore a greater incentive and enthusiasm to participate more fully in the running of the farm.

A good arrangement is one by which the parent can give the child a 'say' in the management of the business or farm, a certain amount of responsibility and a regular income.

Having a Say: A say in business or farm management can be provided simply by the parent making a habit of discussing decisions he / she has had to make with his son/daughter and seeking his/her opinion.

Responsibility: An ideal way for the young farmer to learn how to handle responsibility is for him to have a small enterprise of his own.

Regular Income: Allows the young farmer to maintain the same status as his friends who are getting a regular wage packet.

Partnerships can carry tax implications and also tax breaks which you may find attractive.

Insurance policies can be put in place to protect partners and ensure continuity of the business. Before committing to anything, sit down, and on paper write the answers to some hard questions:
- How will I/my wife/my husband/life partner and family gain from this proposed partnership?
- What are the facts?
- Do I have the capacity to continue this partnership for years to come?
- What can the proposed partner contribute to the business/farm?

- What other options do I have if the partner fails to pull his/her weight in the business/farm?
- Do I have an exit strategy from this partnership if it goes wrong?
- How are profits/ losses to be divided?
- Who will carry responsibility?
- What provision is made for me, my wife/partner and other family members?
- What other options do I have that might give me better peace of mind?

Life Cycle Stages for Succession and Inheritance Planning

AGE	STAGE	PLAN
1	BABY	Parents plan for child's education
5	PRIMARY SCHOOL	Make will
13	TEENAGER	Secondary/Vocational School
15		Parents plan funding for third level education. Update will
17	YOUNG ADULT	Second Level/Third level education
18		Parents and 18 years olds update/make wills
19	FUN AND SPORT	
20	FUN AND SPORT	
21	KEY OF DOOR	Employed/Student
25	NEST BUILDERS 1	Newly Married/Co-Habitees/Partners No children. Young couple start pension plans and are developing their investments.
30	NEST BUILDERS 2	Adult with increasing family. Youngest child under 6.
32	NEST BUILDERS 3	Adult with increasing family Youngest child is 6 or over.
35	PACKED NEST 1	Adult with increasing family. Dependent children. Plan Succession and Inheritance.
40	PACKED NEST 2	Maturing family plan succession and inheritance. All update wills.
42	PACKED NEST 3	Maturing family.
45	LESS NEST 1	Children now away at Secondary School, College or University or in Labour Force. Make Succession plan / Inheritance plans.

50	LESS NEST 2	Succession Plan and Retirement starts. Adjust Retirement plan.
55	EMPTY NEST	Children now independent. Update will.
60	SENIOR 1	Working parents of 30 years ago are now grand parents. Are time rich, modest investments and are still cash poor. Update will / check Retirement plan / Investment plans.
65	SENIOR 2	Now retired. May have special needs for attention, affection and security. Update will / check Retirement plan / Investment plans.
70	SENIOR 3	Having a good time. Increase care / consider passing on assets.
80	SENIOR 4	Having a great time. Update will. Increase care
100	SENIOR 5	Having a wonderful time. Update will.

The Solution

Consider all the options in front of you and get advice. Then choose the option that is best suited to you. It's that simple.

Remember, even whan all the options have been set out, you always have the option of doing nothing and can of course leave things just as they are.

Family Tree

A list of your family members, extended family and friends will help you in deciding on who your beneficiaries and executors may be.

Your family tree or genealogy can help decide ownership and entitlements, distinguish you from others of similar or same names and in cases of estates where administration has not been taken out for generations help you to clear up the estate and bring your affairs up to date.

It becomes especially relevant in situations of cohabitants / partners and where people die without making a will. A developed family tree will provide detail of kinship, bloodline and ancestors. The usual starting point to develop a family tree is investigation of birth certificates, marriage certificates, death certificates, gravestones, church records from which you plot paternal and maternal lines of ancestry. Genealogists, historians and local jornalists may be of help to you in tracing your family tree.

INHERITANCE

When the end of life comes, you will no longer have control of your estate. While you are here, you can do immense good for the next generation.

Check your personal assets list. You can leave a legacy of happiness and prosperity rather than pain and suffering for generations to come.

LAST WILL AND TESTAMENT

I, John Doe, residing at 58 Any Street, Any City, Anywhere do hereby declare this to be my Last Will and Testament and hereby revoke any and all Wills and Codicils at any time heretofore made by me.

I direct that the expenses of my funeral and burial and that my Personal Representative pay such amount as may be required in the applicable law

Making
a Will

You don't have to make a will. However, it is logical to consider leaving your affairs in order for the next generation, or whoever you might like to benefit after you are gone.

This holds true for every stage of life - whether you are a single young adult with few prized possessions, a young parent or a pensioner.

Many Irish people are superstitious and think that if they make a will, they will die. So they avoid the issue altogether. Unless you have access to the fountain of eternal youth or you are immortal, the reality is that like all of us you will at some stage die. Many people die under the age of 30. Yet few would ever have thought about making a will.

If you can accept that, then it is logical that you should consider leaving your affairs in order.

You Decide
On making a will, it is you who decides who gets what after you're gone. You decide who you would like to be your executors and who will ultimately benefit from your estate.

You may wish to benefit your spouse, partner or your children. You may have a child with special needs who will need a little extra care after you are gone. You may want to leave a few euros to a friend, or even give some money to charity. You may wish to give your executors a gift for their work in administering your estate.

By making a will you can provide for each situation. You can set up trusts for children, appoint trustees and appoint guardians. You can also consider carefully the tax implications for each and every person you wish to benefit. Your will may be structured in such a way that it minimises as far as possible the impact of Capital Acquisitions Tax on your beneficiaries.

What if you don't make a will? You are deemed to die 'intestate' and your next of kin will inherit your estate. If you are married with children your spouse will get two thirds (2/3) and your children will get one third (1/3) divided equally between them. If you are not married and have no children your parents will get your estate. In extreme cases, the Irish State is the ultimate intestate successor.

The Succession Act 1965 sets out who gets what. The people who become entitled to your estate are fixed at the very moment of your death and are set out in the table on intestacy on the facing page.

In many cases, the people who ultimately become administrators, and more importantly beneficiaries, are sometimes people whom you would not have wished to benefit at all. You may have someone in your family that you don't get on with or someone who's doing very well for themselves so they don't really need anything from you. If you don't make a will, the wrong people may get it.

Will v. No Will
Example
Eamon and Tara have a farm and dairy business. They have three children. John who farms full-time, Sheila who qualified as a nurse but is now married to Andy and takes fulltime care of their young children and Tom who has done a business degree and is taking 'time out' in Australia.

Will
The parents take time for careful discussion, make wills leaving property to each other, and then they make the following provisions:
1. The farm, entitlements, (rights to EU payments) stock, plus machinery to Tara subject to Eamon paying €50,000 each to Sheila and Tom

2. A site each to Sheila and Tom, to either build for themselves or sell if they wish. (Note-the location of the site is important)

Persons Entitled on Intestacy (No Will)

RELATIVE SURVIVING	DISTRIBUTION OF ESTATE
Spouse and issue	Two thirds to husband; one third equally among the children, with issue of pre-deceased child taking per stirpes.
Spouse and no issue (ISSUE IS THE LEGAL TERM FOR OFFSPRING)	Spouse takes all.
Issue and no spouse	Children take equally with children of a pre-deceased child taking per stirpes.
Father, mother, brothers and sisters	Each parent takes one half.
One parent, brothers and sisters	Parent takes all.
Brothers and sisters	All take equally. Children of a pre-deceased child take per stirpes.
Nephews, nieces and grand-parent	Nephews and nieces take all equally.
Nephews, nieces, uncles, aunts and great grand parents.	Nephews and nieces take all equally.
Uncles, aunts and great grand-parents	Uncles and aunts take all equally.
First cousin, great uncle, great nephew and great, great grand-parent	First cousin, great uncle and great nephew take all equally.

Per Stirpes

Per stirpes is a Latin term so we will explain it in plain English using an example. George had three children, Bill, Bob and Barbara. Bill died in 2002 leaving two children of his own. George died intestate in 2008. Who will take George's estate? Bob and Barbara will take one third each and the remaining one third will be divided equally between Bill's children. That's per stirpes!

3. The residue - anything left in the bank or the lotto if they win it, to be divided equally between John, Sheila and Tom.

No Will

Eamon dies first so his wife Tara gets two thirds of his property and John, Sheila and Tom get one ninth each. But which two thirds, and which one ninth?

As mother (Tara) is still alive, nobody says very much. Some stay quiet out of the genuine respect for a parent, others because they see 'potential'.

Tara just keeps on farming and does it very well with John's assistance. Sheila is living two hours away and visits when she can. Tom has a few more 'oats' to sow, so he returned to Australia. Tara then dies. Her share (two thirds) goes to the children equally so now they have one third each. John is shocked to discover that the farm must be sold.

Sheila is under pressure because Eamonn just lost his job. Tom is easy-going but is not going to walk away from his large inheritance. He is, however, prepared to do a deal with John as he recognises John's commitment over the years to the farm.

Sheila and Andy, however, want their full one third. John is not able to get sufficient borrowing from the bank. The place is sold, John goes looking for work. He and Sheila don't speak again. This is certainly far from what Eamon and Tara intended. Had they both made a will the situation that arose could have been completely avoided.

Survivors Divided

Let's say you are widowed, have five children, a house and don't make a will. When you die, the house will be divided equally between your five children and therefore five people become the owners of the house. This may not be ideal, especially if all the children don't get along.

What's more, if one of your children dies before you die and for example leaves three children of their own, there will then be seven owners of the house. Your four surviving children will take one fifth each and the remaining one fifth will be divided between the three children so they will get one fifteenth each. As you can see, it creates multiple owners and multiple issues.

Now consider that the house has to be sold or work has to still be done. Before anything can happen, each owner has to agree. Failure to agree will be another day's work. Getting seven people to agree may take more than a day's work. Too often, it has taken years in court.

If you make a will, you will enhance the chances of providing a good legacy, avoid expensive courts cases for your next of kin and leave lasting fond memories. The flip side is that you may have been to see your solicitor already. In extreme cases, depending on your own particular circumstances, the best thing to do may be not to make a will at all.

What is a Will?

A will is a document that states in clear terms how you wish your estate, that is your assets or property, to be distributed after your death.

A will is possibly the most important document you may ever sign in your lifetime. Of course you cannot be consulted about when it really comes into effect. That is after your death.

So it's important to get it right.

Definitions

Testator = man who has made or is making will
Testatrix = woman who has made or is making will.

Can you make a Will?

If you have reached 18 and are of sound disposing mind then you can make a will. To make a will therefore involves two things, 1. Age and 2. Capacity.

1. Age

The lower age limit for making a will is 18 but there is no upper age limit.

2. Capacity

You must have the mental capacity to make a will. You must have this capacity both at the date you give your solicitor instructions regarding your will and the date you actually sign it. A testator is presumed to have capacity until the contrary is proven.

To have capacity, you must understand at least the following:
a. that you are disposing of assets on death.
b. that you are fully aware and understand the nature and extent of your assets.
c. that you will be benefiting certain people on your death and you do in fact wish to benefit those people.

If there is doubt about your capacity, a doctor's certificate will usually be called for. If the doctor too has doubts about your capacity, you cannot make a will. The issue of capacity is subjective. Each person is different and while some cases the loss or lack of capacity can be clear, other cases aren't so clear cut.

The Mental Capacity and Guardianship Bill is currently making its way through the Oireachtas. If the Bill becomes law it will put the issue of mental capacity on a statutory footing. It states that 'it shall be presumed until the contrary is established, that every person who has reached the age of majority has full capacity to make a decision affecting him or her'. For more information you can view the Bill on www.oireachtas.ie.

You may be mentally sound. However other issues can cast doubt on your ability to make a will. These are outside or external factors. You must not be unduly influenced or put under any pressure to make a will.

When people go to court, there are no real winners, though in some cases court may be the only option to prevent injustice. A lot of time, effort and money will be used up on legal costs in particular. While going to court is absolutely necessary in some cases, it should be avoided if possible.

If it was proved that a will was made in favour of a particular person by coercion or undue influence, a court can 'strike down' or cancel that will. This may mean that an earlier will shall become activated once again or if there was no earlier will then the person shall be deemed to have died intestate.

Sometimes very sick or elderly people can be vulnerable in the same way that children can be vulnerable. The lower age limit here protects children but there is no similar protection for the elderly. In practice, the solicitor has a responsibility to protect the vulnerable person. Believe it or not in most cases a vulnerable person will be influenced or put under pressure by someone close to them.

What are the requirements for a Will?
A will must have the following basic elements:
- It must be in writing
- It must show a full name and address of the testator or testatrix
- It must revoke any previous will
- A minimum of one executor should be appointed by the testator/testatrix, although two is customary to allow for more transparency
- If the will creates a trust for young children then it must also appoint trustees (and preferably guardians). It should state clearly who is to receive what and which property is to be included in the trust. It should provide all necessary powers to the trustees to enable them to carry out their duties
- A residue clause should always be inserted. This would clarify any unexpected windfalls such as winning the National Lottery
- It should state the date the will is made and that is followed by the signature of the testator or testatrix
- Below the signature an attestation clause is always inserted, showing that the testator

or testatrix signed in the presence of two witnesses. The signatures of those witnesses will be the last thing on the will. *(Section 78 of the Succession Act).*

What if you are blind or can't read or write?
Being illiterate does not prevent you from making a will. The will is usually read over to you, and as long as you understand the contents of the will, you can make a mark in the form of an 'X' or some other mark instead of signing. Alternatively you can direct someone else to sign the will on your behalf.

A blind person can sign a will but if they choose not to, they can also direct someone else to sign on their behalf. While a blind person can obviously make a will, unfortunately they cannot witness one as the Succession Act requires that the witnesses must see the testator signing.

What can you leave by Will?
The law says that a person may by his/her will dispose of all property which he/she is beneficially entitled to at the time of his/her death.

The word 'property' includes all property, whether it's a house, land, money, shares or jewellery, but does not include jointly owned property as joint property will usually pass by 'survivorship' to the other joint owner. Property that is specifically nominated to someone on death would be treated similarly.

So, you must identify clearly both what you have and who you are leaving it to. Any confusion cannot be clarified when you're gone!

But I don't have anything!
You may think you have nothing in this world of any value. However if you sit down and work it out you could soon realise that you may be worth more on death than in life. Do you have an Insurance Policy or a Death in Service benefit? Do you have a car, a house or some old shares that you thought were not worth anything? If you have anything at all no matter how small, you should consider making a will.

Example of a Will
Please do not use this example as a basis for your own will as it may not cover your particular circumstance, no matter how appropriate you think it looks.

If you have a spouse then obviously he or she is your number one choice, unless of course you are separated (still married but no longer living together) or divorced (no longer married).

If you are unhappily divorced you may be thinking about how to prevent your former spouse or his or her family from getting anything from 'your' estate. Did the court give 'mutual blocking orders'?

Let's assume for the moment that everything in the garden is rosy and that you are in a happy marriage or long term relationship. 'I leave everything to my spouse or partner but if she or he dies before me, my estate is to be sold and the proceeds divided amongst all my children'.

Before you go any further with your thinking and planning, have a look at the simple will of one Michael Murphy.

Michael Murphy's Will

This is the last Will and Testament of Michael Murphy of 45 Sydney Walk, Dublin and I hereby revoke all former Wills and Testamentary Dispositions made by me.

I leave all my property to my Wife Mary and I appoint her my Sole Executrix.

Should my Wife Mary predecease me or die within thirty days of my death the following provisions shall apply;

I appoint my children Tom and Nuala as my Executors and I direct them to pay my just debts, funeral and testamentary expenses.

I leave all my property to my said children Tom and Nuala in equal shares share and share alike.

As witness my hand this*** day of **** 200*.

SIGNED PUBLISHED AND DECLARED by the Testator as and for his last Will and Testament in our presence who in his presence and at his request and in the presence of each other have hereunto subscribed our names as witnesses this Will having been printed on the front side only of the foregoing sheet of A.4 paper.

Michael Murphy's will is straight forward but before he put it in place he had carefully discussed all his requirements with his solicitor. He discussed the tax implications too. He took into consideration the value of his property which would be received by his children in the event of his wife's death before him or within 30 days after him.

If for instance Bart and Marguerete have children the estate or property could even be 'scattered' a little further by including their children. By doing this it can lessen the impact on the children of a major tax bill that could mean that it has to be sold to pay the tax bill.

When to make a Will?
When to make a will is entirely up to you. It makes sense to make the will while you are fit and healthy. Don't leave it until you are dying or are panicking at the last minute that you never made a will. This is really not the time to be worried about your will. You probably won't be thinking straight or you might make hasty decisions.

You might feel like you just have to make some sort of a will. Making a will in a hospital when you are battling illness, hooked up to monitors, with family, friends, doctors and nurses running around you, with your solicitor sitting on the end of your bed hand writing your will, is not ideal.

Wills are often made this way but the solicitor must still comply with the rules making sure you have the mental capacity to make a will and watching out to make sure you have not been influenced unduly into making certain decisions.

Your solicitor will be unable to make the will if there is a high risk of lack of mental capacity or that you have been influenced unduly by someone else into making a will or to leaving certain gifts to certain beneficiaries.

Our best advice is write your will sooner rather than later. Don't wait until the last minute. Don't leave an unsatisfactory will. And don't die intestate.

Once you have accumulated any property you should put a will in place. Make the will for today's circumstances. Even though the value of your assets is most likely to increase, don't try to imagine how your circumstances will be in ten years time. None of us can predict the future with any degree of certainty. Review your will when your circumstances change. This could be when you buy or sell property, move house, make an investment and so on.

Can you DIY?
You can of course make your own will. Some bookshops or stationery shops sell do-it-yourself will packs. You can get them on the internet too. Before you go down that road, thinking you are going to save yourself time and money, ask yourself if you can carry through the whole process of writing your will without the guidance of your solicitor.

Solicitors and lawyers in general find that most DIY wills have caused difficulty. Some are badly drafted or worded. The construction of simple words and sentences can convey many different interpretations.

Some wills are not properly signed or witnessed or a beneficiary signs the will in the mistaken belief that beneficiaries had to witness wills. Sometimes these cases end up in court, being challenged by a disgruntled beneficiary or someone else with a desire to see a judge declare the will invalid.

If a DIY or 'home-made' will, or any will for that matter, is found to be invalid, then it is as if you never made a will at all and you will be deemed to have died intestate. The Succession Act then lists the people entitled to the estate and of course this may be the exact opposite to what the testator or testatrix wanted.

Ask yourself if you would:
• service or repair your own car?
• give yourself a tooth filling?
• draw the plans, specifications and build your own house?

If you have answered yes to the above three questions then you might indeed manage to make your own will, understand the legal and tax issues involved and the consequences of providing or failing to provide for spouses, partners and children correctly.

If, like most of us, you entrusted your car to a qualified mechanic, your tooth to a qualified dentist and your home to a good builder or construction engineer, who do it everyday, then it seems wise to also consult a professional when making your will.

There is great sense in the saying that if you are your own doctor you have a fool for a patient. And that is true of doctors and solicitors too. Even a solicitor will go to see another solicitor to make their own will.

Who can you leave it to?
You are free to leave your estate to who ever you wish, but there are some restrictions which are dealt with fully in the next chapter.

If you have a spouse, you can exclude him or her from your will. However, to do so will mean that your spouse will have an automatic right to a share in your estate. This is known as 'the legal right share'. In this case, a legal right share can be a third or a half, depending on whether there are children or not. The legal right share does not arise where the parties are divorced as obviously they are no longer spouses. However if the parties are separated then they are still married and you must ensure that your spouse's Succession Act rights have been blocked in any separation agreement, if that is what you want.

Similarly the legal right share does not arise if the spouse signs a valid renunciation. If you have children and no spouse then you may have a moral duty to make proper provision for those children in accordance with your means in your will if you have not already done so during your lifetime. These issues are delt with in the next chapter.

What if you've already provided for the children?

If you give a child €€10,000 during your lifetime, then depending on your means, you may not be under any obligation to make provision for them, under your will. This is called advancement. If you gave the child €10,000 during your life and you do not want the child to get another €10,000 under your will, simply inform your solicitor that the €10,000 gift is to be taken into account. This means the child won't get it twice. In any event there is a rule against 'double portions', that is if a testator leaves you €10,000 under a will but you already got the €10,000 from the testator while they were alive, then you will not get the bequest under the will.

You may wish them to have the additional €10,000 in your will. This is called the 'clean slate' principle. When you are making your will, inform your solicitor that you have already given your child €10,000 and would like to leave them €10,000 under your will now also. The solicitor will insert a clause stating that 'advancement shall not be taken into account' regarding that child. This means that the child will get both. Parents do this where they may have provided substantial gifts to their children during their lifetimes to help them set up a business get onto the property ladder or perhaps receive a cash gift on getting married.

Difference between a Deed and a Will

A Deed is a document that transfers land or property from one living person to another. Once the transferor signs the deed the job is pretty much done. It only remains for the transferee to pay any stamp duty and the solicitor to register the deed, at which time the transferee becomes the legal owner of the property.

A will is completely different. It is an expression of your intentions as to how and to whom you wish your property to go to after your death. As such it does not take effect until you die. When you leave the solicitor's office having made your will, all the property is still yours to do with as you wish. You can go back and change the will as many times as you wish or you can decide to sell all the assets mentioned in the will.

What is Lapse?

Lapse occurs where the gift in the will fails to take effect. There can be a number of reasons for this. Each will be considered briefly as they are factors to be considered at the time of making your will.

1. Ademption

If you make a will today leaving a house in Cork to your friend, but tomorrow you sell that house and spend the money on a cruise around the world, then the gift, i.e. the house, cannot form part of your estate as it no longer exists and so your friend will receive nothing. If you leave your entire lottery winnings to the Cats and Dogs home but you spend all the money while you are alive there is simply nothing left for the Cats and Dogs home.

Another way in which a gift can be adeemed is where the gift object itself is altered. For example, if you have 500 shares in ABC Company and you leave these under the will you made in 1996 to your daughter. ABC company is subsequently taken over by XYZ Company in 2000 and they issue new shares. So your 500 shares in ABC become 500 shares in XYZ.

On a strict reading of your will your daughter will not get the XYZ shares as these were not left to her under your will. What she got was the shares in ABC. However if the new share issue is simply replacing the old then your daughter will most likely receive the shares.

2. Uncertainty

Where the subject of the gift or the intended beneficiary cannot be identified and there is no evidence to assist the court in identifying either the gift or the beneficiary, the gift will be void because it is uncertain.

It is vital therefore when making your will that you provide your solicitor with full details to enable both the gift and the beneficiary to be clearly identified. The first example of how it can go wrong is: 'I leave my house in Galway to my wife' in circumstances where you have in fact got two houses in Galway.

The other would be: 'I leave my house in Galway to my nephew John' but you have two nephews called John.

In the first example you must sufficiently identify the house by giving the full address and description of the property. In the second example you can identify the nephew you wish to benefit by saying my nephew John, son of my sister Deirdre or as the case may be.

Evidence can be admitted either under the Succession Act section 90 (outside evidence) or section 99 (doubt) to show that you meant to leave a particular house or that you meant to favour a particular nephew. If we are talking about evidence then we are talking about court and that means that there will be legal costs involved in order to establish the correct house or the correct beneficiary.

You can see how easily uncertainty can arise and the potential problems that can ensue by failing to identify people or property correctly in your will. As uncertainty can only be displaced by certainty, you should provide full and accurate details to your solicitor to ensure that the correct information is recorded in your will. Get it right at the outset and both court and costs can be avoided.

3. Beneficiary as a witness

Where a beneficiary (or their spouse or any person claiming under them) witnesses a will they will not be able to benefit under that will.

For example, you leave €5,000 to your son in your will and he also signs his name as a witness. His witnessing of the will is grand but unfortunately he will not receive the €5,000. Witnesses are simply not allowed to benefit. This is due to the obvious risks that the witness may have exerted some form of influence or pressure over the testator.

The problem of a beneficiary witnessing the will can be corrected by a codicil (see below), which of course will also to be signed and witnessed in the same manner as a will. You can confirm the gift to the beneficiary and have two different people witness the codicil, with the result that the beneficiary will receive the gift.

Can you prevent a gift from lapsing?

There is a way to prevent a gift from lapsing. If someone dies before you then they are not around to receive whatever you have left them in your will. If for example you are divorced or widowed and you decide to leave your estate between your children, this can be important.

For example, you make your will in 2006. You have three children to divide your estate amongst Tom Dick and Harry. They are all married with children of their own. But let's say Tom died in 2007 and then you die without having changed your will to take account of his death. In this case the one third share that Tom would have received had he survived, would lapse. However because Tom had children of his own, thanks to Section 98 of the Succession Act, the gift is saved and does not lapse. Instead, the gift will pass into Tom's estate. If Tom made a will it will pass to whomever he has left his estate to under his will.

Testators must be aware of this where they have grandchildren but in particular they should be aware as to what will happen if a child dies before them as sometimes the daughter or son in law may not be the preferred beneficiary. If Tom died intestate, then it will pass to those entitled on intestacy.
(Section 98 of the Succession Act)

Death of Beneficiary

If a beneficiary under your will dies shortly after you, but prior to receiving their inheritance under your will, then the gift will not lapse but instead it will pass into the deceased beneficiary's estate. It will then be distributed in accordance with their will.

What is a Codicil?

A codicil is document which is made in the same way as a will. It is used to make small changes to a will. It does not revoke a will but rather it is kept with it. When you die, the will and the codicil are looked at as one document. It is really only used for small changes but if a more comprehensive review of your will is being carried out it is better to make a new will.

Revoking your Will

The only situation where a will is automatically revoked is the subsequent marriage of the testator or testatrix. The exception to this is where the will has been made in contemplation of a specific marriage. It cannot be made in contemplation of marriage generally.

The Succession Act, Section 85 sets out conditions for the revocation of a will. For example:

'. Tim made his will six months ago. Shortly afterwards, he had a row with the beneficiary. He went to his solicitor's office and collected his will. He took it home and wrote 'revoked' across it and threw it in to the top drawer of his desk. On his death the will is discovered. Has it been revoked? Surprisingly the answer is No. Such a revocation would only have had effect if it was signed by Tim and done in the presence of two witnesses. The same capacity to make a will is required to revoke it. However, when revoking a will you or someone at your directions must tear or burn or otherwise destroy the will.

Every time you make a new will you will see that it commences with the words 'this is the last Will and Testament of me .... and I hereby revoke all former Wills and Testamentary dispositions made by me'.

What if your Will is Lost?

If a will is lost and cannot be traced on the death of the testator and the will is last known to be in the possession of the testator then the law will presume that the testator destroyed it. As this is a 'presumption' it can be rebutted but very weighty evidence would be needed. However if a copy of the will can be found, evidence of the contents of the will can be admitted to probate provided the court is satisfied that a diligent search was made for the original will. The reason a copy can be admitted to probate is because the law actually prefers that a person dies testate as opposed to intestate.

If an original will is lost and a copy cannot be found on the death of the testator, the testator is deemed to have died intestate and the estate will be divided up between those entitled.

A full search must of course be conducted and all local solicitors must be asked whether they hold an original will for the deceased. An advertisement must also be placed in the Law Society Gazette which is circulated to all solicitors in the country to ask if any of them have knowledge of the whereabouts of the original will of the deceased.

Some countries have a wills register which is a record that you have made a will. Ireland doesn't have such a register.

Absence of a Beneficiary

Apart from identifying clearly who your beneficiaries are, you should also inform your solicitor of their whereabouts. An exact address or contact telephone number will always help but if they can't be traced it will be necessary to place advertisements in newspapers in the area which they were last known to live.

If they still can't be traced then the share that they are entitled to from your estate can either be lodged in Court or held by the solicitor for a period of seven years. The reason for the seven year period is that if a person cannot be traced within that time there is a presumption that they are dead. Sometimes it is necessary to obtain a Court Order to proceed with distribution of the estate in the absence of a beneficiary. This will only result in additional costs not to mention delay in distributing your estate.

Storage of your Will

Most solicitors have a fire proof wills safe in which wills are stored. They do not charge for storage. A copy is always given to the testator or testatrix. If you make and pay for your will, it is your document so you can take it home, store it in a bank or some other place of your choosing.

If you store it yourself do make sure you don't lose it, mark it, tear it or clip anything to it as this can cause problems with the probate office when it comes to having your will admitted to probate.

How much does it Cost?

Some solicitors charge nothing for making a will and some charge €2,000 or more. Some will throw the making of your will in for free if you are doing another legal transaction at the same time. Much depends on how complicated your will is likely to be. The reality is, in 2008, most solicitors will charge in the region of €200 to make a standard will which is usually a lot less than the real cost of the time involved, particularly when the responsibility factor is taken into account.

How long will it take to Organise?

Some wills such as the 'hospital will', the 'home from America for two days will' or ' the going on holidays tomorrow will' are more urgent than others. The solicitor may visit the hospital or the person home from America.

For most wills, you visit your solicitor, say what you have and who you would like to leave it to. The solicitor advises you, drafts the will and a few days later sends it out to you for approval. When you have considered the contents of the draft will, you make an appointment to go back to see your solicitor to sign it. It's that simple! Believe it or not, you can actually plan your will in less than 15 minutes - the time it takes to boil a kettle and make and drink a cup of tea.

Here's how:

First,   get a pen and a sheet of paper and sit down at the kitchen table.

Second,   using the My Assets list as a guide, write down on that sheet of paper a short list of what you own.

Third,   pick up the phone and phone your solicitor's office and make an appointment.

Fourth,   keep the appointment whether it's at the solicitor's office or at your home. That's it!

Conclusion
Everyone should make a will irrespective of circumstances. It may be the most important document you ever sign.

Guidenote: If you are to take only one idea from this book, it is make a will. Make your will for today's circumstances. Do not try to imagine how you think circumstances will be in 10 years time. None of us have a crystal ball so we can't really predict the future with any degree of certainty. Just make the will.

If there are any major changes in your life, review your will. Your solicitor will tell you if it needs to be changed. One way or the other, review your will every two to four years to take any changes in the law or in tax legislation into account.

Guidenote: Witnesses to the signing of a will are usually members of the solicitor's staff, so you don't need to bring any witness with you.

A Difference
One word in a will can make all the difference. Read the sentence: 'I wish to give all my land to the Cats and Dogs Home and my nephew John'.

Now compare it with the sentence: 'I want all my lands to be sold and the proceeds given to the Cats and Dogs Home and my nephew John'.

The result of using the word 'give' would mean that the estate would be given to the beneficiaries and they could argue among themselves what best to do with it e.g. divide it into parcels of equal area. This could lead to disputes over an estate that might have properties in different countries.

Which beneficiary gets which property? Which beneficiary gets which field or which house? If the stipulation is that it be 'sold', then the estate would ideally be sold by public auction and the value of the estate would be divided in money terms equally.

Asserting Legal Rights of
Spouses and Children

If you make a will you can leave whatever you like to whoever you like. This is called 'freedom of testation'. You can leave it all to charity, to science or to the cats and dogs home if you wish. But, as always, nothing is ever that straight-forward.

Freedom of Testation is something we inherited from the English. Up to the 1960s a testator was free to dispose of his property as he saw fit. We say 'he' because back then assets were usually in the man's name. A consequence of that freedom was that he was the 'bread winner' and he could be as arbitratory and capricious in his will as he pleased. As long as he was mentally competent the court would not intervene to 'change' his will. even if it left his family in dire straits.

History
However in the 1960s when the Succession Bill was making its way through the Dáil and Seanad, Mr. Charles J. Haughey TD, the then Minister for Justice argued that the right to disinherit a spouse in a family was unacceptable and that there was no real basis, moral or historical for the view that it was acceptable. It was argued that as far back as Roman Law, freedom of testation was

considerably restricted and a man could not simply do as he pleased with his estate. Well the Romans never made it to Ireland, however their laws and traditions were discussed in the Dail debates on the Succession Bill. At the time the legislators looked also to European Law, as throughout Europe particularly in the 'civil code' systems, limits were placed on testamentary freedom by providing a fixed share of the deceased's estate for the surviving spouse and children.

The Constitution was also a factor. The Minister argued that in the context of this constitutional view of the family, freedom of testation was an indefensible paradox which was heightened by Article 41 of the Constitution, which recognises the support which a married woman gives to the State by her life within the home, without which the common good could not be achieved; the State for its part undertaking to ensure that mothers should not be obliged, by economic necessity, to engage in labour to the neglect of their duties in the home.

Such a principle, it was argued, could not be reconciled in a system of law which allowed a man to disinherit his spouse and leave his property to strangers. It was simply no longer acceptable.

The Succession Act
The Succession Act was enacted in 1965 and it was brought into effect on 1 January 1967. It is now over 40 years old and remains relatively unchanged. It tried to do what a man was expected or supposed to do, to provide for his spouse and children on his death. It gives to the surviving spouse a fixed share of the deceased spouse's estate.

It also gives to a surviving child the right to apply to the Court for provision to be made out of the deceased's estate on the ground that the parent has failed in their moral duty to make proper provision for that child in accordance with his or her means. The child's entitlements, unlike the surviving spouse, are not automatic and must be asserted.

It may be unthinkable today but there were times when husbands had deliberately excluded their wives from their will. This may have happened for a variety of reasons. The wife may have already been adequately provided for by the husband during his lifetime, she may have been wealthy in her own right, he may have wanted to benefit his children directly, or he didn't want her to get her hands on 'his' money. He may not have liked his wife or they may have just been together for the children. Back then, he didn't need a reason. He just left it to whoever he wanted and the law didn't intervene.

Spouses – How things are Today
The legal right share is found in Section 111 of the Succession Act 1965 and it provides:
1. If a testator leaves a spouse and no children, the spouse shall have a right to one half of the estate.

2. If the testator leaves a spouse and children, the spouse shall have a right to one third of the estate.

What's yours is Mine....

It is best shown by an example. Sheila and James are married and have one child. Sheila makes a will and leaves her house worth €230,000 and her bank account which has €10,000 in it, to her cousin Joe in America. In this case because James has been left nothing, his legal right share arises automatically. As they have a child, James is entitled to receive a one third share of Sheila's estate.

Decisions, Decisions....

Taking the above example a little further, if Sheila by her will, leaves James the €10,000 in the bank, but still leaves the house to her cousin, then James must elect, or choose, between taking the €10,000 left to him in the will or taking his legal right share. Again, as they have a child, he is entitled to a third of her estate, which would be €80,000.

He must decide what he wants. If he decides to take his legal right share, then the estate must cough up. Now, it may well be the case that even though the bequest under the will is worth €70,000 less than what his legal right share would be, he may elect to simply take the bequest under the will and so the house will go to her cousin as planned.

Sheila's executors have a duty to notify James, in writing, of his right of election. He must elect within six months from the date on which he was first notified or alternatively one year from the date the Grant of Probate is taken out in Sheila's estate, whichever is later. Time is hugely important here. If he doesn't choose within the time frame then he will get the €10,000 under the Will and that's that. However if he elects to take his legal right share, which would be €80,000, he can take the €10,000 left to him in the Will in partial satisfaction.

The legal right share has priority over and above rights of creditors of the deceased.

Home Sweet Home....
The Constitution of Ireland (Bunreacht na hÉireann) affords essential personal and property rights for the 'family' and the 'dwelling'. The Succession Act took this a step further by providing the surviving spouse with the right to acquire the family home in which she had lived. This was provided for in Section 56(1) of the Succession Act. Where the estate of a deceased person includes a house in which at the time of the deceased's death, the surviving spouse was residing, the surviving spouse may require the legal personal representatives (LPRs) to appropriate the house in or towards satisfaction of the share of the surviving spouse'. This provides even further protection to the surviving spouse in that they will not be forced to leave the home in which they have lived even though it has not been left to them.

What's more, the spouse can also require the personal representatives to appropriate any household chattels in or towards her share. Household chattels include furniture, linen, china, glass, books, garden effects and domestic animals. Similarly, rights under Section 56 must be notified to the spouse in writing by the LPRs.

Remember, where property is held jointly between the spouses, it passes automatically by survivorship, i.e. outside the terms of a will and so the surviving spouse doesn't have to worry about appropriating the dwelling.

When is a Spouse not a Spouse?
Separation
Unfortunately, spouses sometimes separate. The numbers are increasing. Many separate informally and never go to see a solicitor. They just start living separate and apart. Others prefer to have a separation agreement drawn up with a solicitor or if they cannot agree on terms of separation, they can get a court ordered separation. In these cases Succession Act rights can and usually are 'blocked' even though the parties are still husband and wife. Separation ends the relationship but it does not end the marriage.

The separated spouse is still a spouse and so he or she is entitled to apply to court to have further provision made for them from the deceased spouse's estate. The court can of course extinguish the Succession Act rights altogether but if it is not satisfied that the proper provision has been made for the separated spouse, it can order that further provision be made from the deceased's estate now. If you are already separated you really have to be aware of these provisions when making your will.

Divorce

As part of the Divorce Order, each spouse can also have Succession Act rights 'blocked'. Once a divorce is granted however, the spouses are no longer spouses and each is free to re-marry. If either spouse has a will made, it should be changed immediately. In both cases you should remember that in having such rights blocked, a court would always have to be satisfied that adequate and reasonable financial provision has already been made for the spouse where necessary.

In a divorce situation the right to apply to court is available also, even though the spouses are no longer married. However, if the surviving former spouse has re-married then an application to court cannot be made. Again, in a divorce situation, Succession Act rights can and usually are, blocked to prevent such applications being made.

Foreign Divorce

Prior to 1996 many Irish couples went abroad to obtain a divorce. Many didn't realise that there are specific rules relating to foreign divorce particularly residency and domicile. Later, perhaps one or other of these divorced spouses may have re-married. No doubt when making a will, any reference to 'my spouse' by the deceased would have meant the spouse from the second marriage. However if the first divorce was not valid then the subsequent second marriage similarly cannot be valid.

As you can see this can give rise to huge problems from both an inheritance and tax point of view. It is vital when giving your solicitor instructions in relation to your will that you inform them of any previous marriages or divorces and where they took place. It would also be helpful if you could provide them with copies of previous marriage certificates and/or divorce papers. Any problems regarding marital status cannot be fixed when you are gone.

Pas pour moi merci (Not for me thanks…)

A spouse can relinquish any rights or entitlements they may have to their spouses' estate. This is called 'a renunciation'. Such a renunciation must be in writing, it must be done during the lifetime of the deceased spouse and the spouse renouncing must be independently advised by a solicitor as they are giving up valuable rights. Believe it or not, spouses sometimes sign renunciations to appease their partner, or they may not need or want anything from their partner's estate. People who have re-married after a divorce or who have been widowed sometimes sign renunciations in order to benefit the children of the first or former marriage. More often than not, where one spouse signs a renunciation, the other will do so too.

'Till death do us part...

'Unworthiness to succeed' is covered by Section 120 of the Succession Act. This means that for reasons mentioned below the surviving spouse may not be entitled to benefit under the deceased spouse's estate whether they left a will or not. If there is a will they may be precluded from making any assertion or taking any entitlement under that will.

The circumstances are as follows:

1. Where a spouse has been found guilty of the murder, attempted murder or manslaughter of the other.
2. Where a Decree of Divorce *a mensa et thoro* (A court order given to one person relieving them of the obligation to reside with the other) has been obtained.
3. Where a spouse has failed to comply with a Decree of Restitution of conjugal rights obtained by the deceased.
4. Where a spouse guilty of desertion that has continued up to the death of the deceased spouse for two years or more.
5. Where a person found guilty of an offence against the deceased or against the spouse or any child of the deceased including a person to whom the deceased was in loco parentis (in place of a parent) at the time of the offence.

There are provisions in place to prevent a testator from substantially disinheriting their spouse. Section 121 of the Succession Act states that any disposition (transfer or sale) of property made within three years of the testator's death, can be set aside by a court, if the court is satisfied that the disposition was made for the purpose of disinheriting the spouse or children.

If a court is satisfied that a person transferred property to a beneficiary within the three years before his or her death, in the hope that the spouse would not get the property, then the court can set aside the transfer and order that the property once again forms part of the deceased person's estate.

The person who received the property will be none too happy but the law will not allow a deliberate attempt by a person to disinherit their spouse or children.

Guidenote: Where a spouse takes the legal right share, this will impact on the other beneficiaries in the will and they may not get what they expected. Spouses are completely exempt from inheritance tax.

CHILDREN

Most families fail the ideal family test. In an ideal family, there will never be arguments. Common sense and understanding will prevail in spite of injustice. Such an ideal is a myth. The only thing about common sense is that it isn't very common.

Take an example: Daddy has died. He has left his entire fortune to his eldest son. Out

of the blue, the youngest son protests. He is enraged and feels that his big brother does not deserve the fortune. He will sue. He will take a case to court. He will claim against his father's estate.

When planning your will, your solicitor will ask you a series of questions. One such question is: 'When you die, will any family member be upset with your will?' In other words, 'Is anyone likely to sue your estate?'

Section 117 of the Succession Act gives certain rights to children. These rights arise where a parent fails in his / her moral duty to make proper provision for a child, either during their lifetime or on death, in accordance with their means. In recent years the increase in values of property and wealth has been mirrored by an increasing number of claims by children against parents' estates.

There are two perspectives here, that of the parent and that of the child. Most parents will try to provide for their children as best they can and to be as fair as possible when it comes to dividing the assets among the children. To provide for children is instinctive. However, sometimes parents decide to exclude certain children perhaps because of the child's 'easy come, easy go' attitude to money or perhaps because the child is going through a divorce and to leave assets to them may mean that the divorcing spouse would be entitled to a share.

A person has the right to protect their assets as they see fit. In other instances, a son may be doing very well in his own right or you may have given a daughter a large cash gift in recent years to set her up in a house or business. When planning your will try to consider whether anyone will be offended or upset by the will that you leave.

Let's say you have three children, all of whom have worked the business or farm with you for many years. Is it conceivable that two will be upset if you leave the business or farm to one? The answer is obviously yes. The view of the parent might be 'the business or farm is too small to carve it up between three'. The views of the children might be, 'why did he leave it all to him' or 'why did he leave us out, does he not love us?' While some issues are glaringly obvious and can easily be dealt with when your will is being drafted, some are less so and if all issues are not fully explored by the solicitor and divulged by the parent when the will is being drafted, the estate could face costly litigation.

Must be Asserted

A child's rights do not arise automatically. They must be asserted. Unlike a spouse's rights, if there is no provision in the will for a child, the child has to sue the parents' estate for provision to be made for them. The child can of course be male or female, five or fifty five. For a minor child (a child under 18) the claim can be brought by a guardian or someone else in loco parentis.

A child cannot sue just because they've been left out. It's much more complex than that. There must be a failure by the parent to make provision for the child. The parents' means have to be considered. The child's position in life, their health and financial prospects and whether the parent has already provided for them, are all factors that come under the scrutiny of the court. The behaviour of the child towards the parent and vice versa can also be a factor. In recent times the courts have hardened their attitude towards these cases and now a child must show that they have a real and genuine 'need' which could and should have been satisfied by the parent, but wasn't.

What can parents do....
Full disclosure

When you are drafting your will, clearly identify all children including those born of marriage, outside of marriage, adopted, fostered and step-children. Include all other dependents that you may have. By providing full and detailed information to your solicitor you will get full and detailed advice. By not disclosing important information regarding dependants you are rendering the advice useless.

Advancement

Depending on the number of children you have and your available resources, you may wish to give a particular child or children a gift of money right now. This is called 'advancement'. Any gifts given to the child during the parents' lifetime will be taken into account when it comes to them receiving an inheritance from you. In fact, any advancement made to a child shall, subject to any contrary intention, be taken as being so made in or towards satisfaction of the child's share of the estate.

This can help to prevent a claim against your estate, if it can be shown that you have already

provided for your children. When you are drafting your will and if you wish to have the slate wiped clean on your death, you may insert a provision into your will to say that advancement shall not be taken into account. Otherwise the presumption of advancement will apply.

Equal Shares

If you leave your estate to all children in equal shares then this too can help guard against claims as it is obvious that you are trying to be as fair as possible. The problem is, some children require more help than others.

Needy Children

One child might be down on luck or poorly educated with less prospects in life than your other children. You may have a child with special needs in which case you might want to divert a larger chunk of your estate into a trust to provide for that child in which case, the other children will usually understand.

When can a child not sue?

A claim can be brought only where there is a valid will. If the parent has made no will, there is nothing to challenge as all the children will receive a set share of the estate under the intestacy provisions, which are set in the chapter on making a will. Where the surviving spouse has been left the entire estate, and that spouse is the parent of the child, the child cannot bring a claim. If the surviving spouse however is not the parent of the child, e.g., the child is a child of a previous marriage, then in this case the child can bring a claim under Section 117.

Since the Divorce Act in 1996, there is a strict time limit of six months from the date of the Grant of Probate in which the child must bring their claim. The time will not be extended no matter how unfortunate the child's circumstances might be. It cannot be extended by disability, by age or otherwise. As such, it can work very unfairly against minor or disabled children. If your father has just left your brother the house, the car and the bank account and you don't think it's fair you should stop reading this right now. Pick up the phone and make an appointment with your solicitor. The clock is already ticking.

Essentials
If you exclude a child from your will or treat one child differently from others, your solicitor should record the reason and keep this record with your will. Your reasons may be very important in the event of a child suing your estate.

Some parents think that once they treat their children equally the estate is invulnerable to a Section 117 claim. It is not. It can only help to guard against a claim. Section 117 is not about equality between children. It is about making provision for children.

A Child Executor
If you are divorced or widowed you may wish to appoint a child as an executor in your will. This normally doesn't cause a problem but if you then leave your entire estate to a different child it can cause a difficulty because the child to whom you have left nothing may decide to sue your estate. That child will have to renounce their position as executor.

This will mean you have no executor to defend the case. It will also mean that someone else, probably the child that has been left everything, will have to step in to take out a Grant of Probate.

Tax impact of variations or settlements of S117 cases
You must also consider inheritance tax and stamp duty. If a Section 117 application is threatened and the family decide to vary the terms of the Will in order to prevent the application, this variation will carry tax and stamp duty consequences.

If proceedings are brought by the child and then settled or determined by the court, the child will be treated for tax purposes as receiving the benefit from the deceased parent and not from other family members. The date of any settlement can be a valuation date for inheritance tax purposes and any tax liability arising must be paid within four months. It is vital that these various dates of inheritance and valuation dates are firstly identified and subsequently agreed in any settlement.

Court Costs
Litigation of any kind is expensive. In litigation it's usually the loser pays the costs. In Section 117 claims however, at least until recently, it was almost 'a given' that the child wouldn't

have to pay costs, irrespective of whether they won or lost the case. This nearly encouraged claims as children had absolutely nothing to lose by taking a claim.

In recent times the courts have hardened their attitude towards these cases and now a child must show that they have a real and genuine 'need' which could have been satisfied by the parent, but wasn't. Costs are no longer guaranteed, it is up to the judge on the day, but be warned. You do not 'automatically' get your costs from the estate. You may have to pay.

Conclusion

If a child is successful against the estate, it will affect the other beneficiaries under the will. Guard against it as best you can. Discuss everything with your solicitor. Omissions can be costly. Remember, the costs of the winners and losers may have to be borne by the estate. If you value your estate do you really want to see a large chunk of it going on legal costs when it could be better spent on education, or setting a child up in business? Of course you don't. Plan ahead.

The Problem

Joan: *Well we'd need to make a family settlement here first.*

Ben: *I don't know. Nowadays a girl walks up the aisle to marry and not alone does she get the man but she gets half a farm as well.*

Joan: *Well you own the farm so from that point of view there is no problem.*

Ben: *I don't like parting with it. That's the problem.*

-From the play *Setting the Inheritance Scene* by Michael Doyle, South East Radio / Camross Drama Group.

Understanding
Family Law &
Relationships

Many relationships break down. Breakdown may be a factor in any succession or inheritance planning. When relationships break down they can also involve dissolution of business partnerships or companies. Sometimes these breakdowns are resolved amicably. Sometimes they are resolved with recourse to the courts. Marriage and partnership breakdowns can be ended or resolved in different ways.

Reconciliation and Counselling

When partners fall out, is the business or the marriage worth saving? Very often the answer is yes. Frequently people become entrenched in the idea of fault whether commercial or marital. Why not take help from an outsider such as a mediator or counsellor who is trained at facilitating discussion and exploring what each person feels the problems are and how they might be resolved? It's surely worth a try.

Mediation

Mediation is probably the most talked about but also the most underused and misunderstood resource for resolution of many disputes.

In commercial disputes the protagonists and their legal teams might appear before the mediator. The mediator has great flexibility in talking to either both sides together or perhaps one side on its own. A mediator may talk with perhaps one party without the lawyer being present or perhaps just with one of the lawyers without anyone else being present. It is all very flexible and completely confidential.

In family mediation it is usual that the clients only attend the mediator. A lot then depends on the skill of the mediator and obviously the mediator must be in touch with Family Law Court practice.

Collaborative Law
Collaborative law is a new concept in Ireland. The idea is that the disputing or aggrieved parties and their lawyers agree to collaborate. In other words they agree to meet together and discuss and try and resolve the issues affecting the parties.

There is a catch however. If the issues are not resolved then neither lawyer can act for the client if the case is to go forward to a court hearing. So the parties could end up with two new sets of lawyers. This obviously leads to greater costs.

In our view, the lawyer has a responsibility to explore all possibilities of settlement of a client's action. If this was done in the ordinary way in family law cases it should result in fewer cases going as far as court.

Three Simple Steps
The following three step approach should keep most Family Law matters out of court except for the formalities. Those cases that still end up in court were probably inevitably going to end up there anyway.

1. Make it obligatory that parties attend before a mediator for three sessions before they consult their lawyers or commence proceedings.

2. Whether the mediation succeeds or fails, the parties can then go to their lawyers either to implement the agreed mediation or to commence legal proceedings for separtation or divorce.

   By commencing and assembling documents for the legal proceedings the lawyers should be obliged to meet early in play to openly discuss settlement, all done on what's called a 'without prejudice' basis.

3. The case then proceeds to court, either just to implement the formalities of an agreed settlement or to have the case heard by a judge if all efforts at mediation and settlement have failed.

Children and Access

You need a licence for a TV, a car, a dog and to catch a fish. But you need no licence to have a child.

Examples:

1. Mary feels she knows what's best for her own five year old child. Mary has just broken up with her partner who is the child's father. The father and indeed his mother (Granny T) have had daily contact with the child since she was born. Mary refuses the father access and he has to go to court to seek access.

2. Granny T also has to go to court to seek access to her grandchild. Mary attends in court when Granny is making her application and tells the judge she has no objection to Granny T visiting.

   The Access Order is made in favour of Granny T. When Granny T goes to exercise the access Mary refuses, Granny T has to go to court again and this time Mary says the child gets upset. The judge in the District Court gives no reason for it but refuses to enforce his own Access Order thus, as far as Granny T is concerned, making a farce out of the law.

   Granny T has to make a number of further court applications before she begins to get anywhere. Meanwhile, even though Mary does not allege anything 'bad' as between the child and the child's father, the judge decides he will wait for the Social Worker's Report before he makes any Order. Everyone knows that the Social Services Report will not arrive for about six months. Meanwhile the child's father has no access.

3. Catriona discovers that her husband John is having an affair and to make it worse it turns out to be with her best friend. She is extremely hurt and confronts him about it and following their discussions it is clear there is no future for their marriage.

   Catriona is hurt and confused and at times more than a little angry. She seeks legal advice. Her solicitor explains the principles of Separation and Divorce, Custody and Access, Maintenance and Property division. He also refers her to mediation. From the outset Catriona and John work out access arrangements themselves.

   Although she is aware that some people 'play the system' she would not even consider denying John access to the children. She knows she could hurt John by being awkward about this but as far as she is concerned it is not a matter for her to give or refuse access. She feels that it is a matter of the children's right of access to both their mother and their father.

These examples are from real life situations.

Throughout Family Law legislation you will hear judges, barristers and solicitors say the words 'in the best interests of the children'. Many people 'play the system' without any proper regard for the 'best interests of the children'. Unfortunately sometimes, they get away with it. The victory is 'hollow'. Children grow up very quickly and learn about what happened. This can rebound very easily in later life on the parent who refused access.

Cross Cultural Relationships
The Irish diaspora are scattering all over the world and understand the needs and concerns of non-nationals who come to Ireland to better themselves, even if only by earning good money which they send or bring home to their own families.

Integration should not mean an amorphous mass of different nationalities all doing the same thing. It should mean that all nationalities adhere to the laws of Ireland. It should also mean that an understanding of different cultures becomes part of our education for children and adults.

Pre-Marriage Counselling
In the context of this discussion on family law and relationships, pre-marriage counselling or pre-relationship counselling is all the more necessary if the relationship is going to be a 'cross cultural' relationship.

Love is blind and sometimes it endures. Young people of all nations and colours like to have a good time and have no particular agenda when meeting each other except having fun.

It is however amazing how entrenched people can become once the partnership is 'cemented' by having a child. Suddenly the culture of the homeland, whether that is Ireland or some other country, is given great importance and can lead immediately to friction and tension as to which partner's culture or religion will be chosen for the child.

The Law was a Milch Cow
A working woman was worth three milch cows. A good cow was worth 25 pieces of silver. A wife was worth half the value of her husband.

The Brehon Laws of Ireland from the 5th to the 12th century gave a value to everything and instead of punishment for a crime there was restorative justice. The injured party got his or her money's worth in value of cows or cattle or other material goods.

Brehon Law allowed a woman to own property in her own right. A marriage could exist for a year to allow you to decide if you were compatible. At the end of that year you could end the marriage and the wife could take back her dowry.

Law was made by a group of brehons or judges. The only court at the time was one of 150 kings in Ireland who handed out their own version of justice.

In the Ireland of the 5th and 6th centuries, men could have a number of wives. Property was a priority in marriage. In cases where the wife contributed no property, the husband could act without his wife's consent. But he had to provide for his wife. If he married into land, his wife held the reins of power.

The Brehon Laws have influenced Irish law on property up to the 1960s to the introduction of the 1965 Succession Act by then minister for justice Charles J. Haughey TD even though English law has dominated from the 12th to the 20th Century.

A Matter of Trust

Let's start with an example which illustrates the need for creating a Trust in some situations.

Grainne's Story

Grainne was born with the genetic disorder of Down Syndrome. Her parents Tom and Mary had actively participated for many years with their local Community Workshop where Grainne was very popular as a client.

Tom and Mary kept their private worries about Grainne's future to themselves and never got around to making wills.

Tom died. The family home was in joint names and so when Tom died Mary automatically became the sole owner. Mary in turn died without making a will. Under the laws of intestacy, Grainne was then the sole person entitled to the family home. She was still attending the Community Workshop daily and was very happy there.

Incapable of Managing

Because of her disability, the law considers Grainne to be incapable of managing her own affairs. As her parents had made no will, her elderly uncle Mike consulted the family solicitor and had to arrange for Grainne to be made a Ward of Court.

The Wards of Court office is a branch of the High Court and her uncle had to be appointed as the 'Committee' of Grainne and all dealings with her assets had to be carefully recorded and scrutinised by the Wards of Court office. This will remain an ongoing responsibility for uncle Mike and the Wards of Court office with assistance from the family solicitor.

Grainne has two cousins Joe and Neil who have always been very close to her. If Tom and Mary had made wills they could have appointed Joe and Neil as trustees and could have set up a trust for Grainne's benefit. It would not have been necessary to involve the Wards of Court office at all.

Would have Saved

The trustees could have been given wide powers in the will to do all things necessary for Grainne's benefit and the trustees could have continued with the job without the necessity for ongoing supervision by the Wards of Court Office. They would have saved on the considerable costs and expenses which eat into the value of the estate.

Grainne herself cannot make a will. When she dies, whatever is left in the estate will be scattered to various next of kin in accordance with intestacy rules.

We'll never Know

If Tom and Mary had taken advice from their solicitor at an early stage and if they had made wills they could have stated in the wills that any funds remaining in the Trust following Grainne's death would go perhaps to the two cousins Joe and Neil or perhaps their families as the people who were closest to Grainne.

Perhaps Tom and Mary would have wanted any surplus left over to go for the benefit of the Local Community Workshop where Grainne had spent so many happy years. Now we'll never know what they would have wanted to be their best possible legacy.

Parent's Worries

May Gannon of Down Syndrome Ireland has stated that the concerns and worries of parents of disabled children are mainly: Who will listen to the wishes and respect the rights of my son or daughter when I no longer can? Who will put my wishes into action? Will the benefits my son / daughter receives from Government be affected by what I leave to him / her? A good legal provision will: Replace fear of the future with a faith in the future. Shed light on the legal, financial and practical solutions for the future. Help the parents let go and relieve the worries of the person who has Down Syndrome.

What is a Trust?

A trust is an arrangement in which a person (the trustee) holds assets (the trust property), for the benefit of another person or persons (the beneficiaries). The word 'settlor' is used to describe the person who decides to put the trust in place. In Grainne's story, the parents Tom and Mary, if they had set up a trust, would be the settlors.

The subject matter of the trust would be their house and possibly all other property. The Trustees could have been Joe and Neil. Grainne of course would have been the beneficiary.

Choosing the Trustees

Who will you choose as your trustees? The simplest answer is - people you can trust. The trustees can be the same as your executors. It really depends on what you require the trustees to do.

If for instance you own a house with your wife and you have very young children, you both just want your trustee to hold onto everything until your children grow up and then divide everything equally. Usually an uncle or aunt, brother or sister would be a suitable trustee in that case.

If, however, you are putting large sums of money aside, you might consider appointing a professional trustee, maybe a solicitor or accountant or fund management firm to deal with that. There will be charges and you must check what they are.

It would be possible for your brother or sister as trustees to take professional advice on fund management but this will involve their time. If you build in provisions for remuneration of your family trustees, it may seem fair but may be a waste of resources if they are not really equipped to manage the trust fund. There are things which need discussion with a trusted adviser.

Trusts can be very important when it comes to protecting your assets. They are also a great way of providing for children under 18, children or adults suffering from a mental or physical disability or they can be used as a method of providing for a beneficiary who might not be so good at managing money, a beneficiary who has large debts or even a beneficiary who is going through a separation or divorce.

Who can you Trust?

Trustees must obviously be people you can trust. No one in their right mind would appoint as trustees, people they didn't trust. They must be over 18 and mentally capable and indeed willing to carry out the duties of a trustee. A person who has been declared a bankrupt or who has been convicted of a crime of dishonesty cannot be a trustee. Nor can a person who has been disqualified as acting as a director under the companies acts.

Powers and Duties of a Trustee

You can appoint three or four trustees, but a minimum of two is required. The Trustee Acts represent the main source of legislation covering and governing trustees. The Succession Act also gives certain powers to trustees where a trust is created by will.

Sometimes the legislation doesn't provide the trustees with all the powers they need to enable them to carry out their duties. You can give a trustee additional powers if you wish and they can be as broad or as narrow as you like. You can grant them powers to invest, to sell, to borrow, or do anything you deem necessary with the trust property for them to carry out their duties. In relation to duties, trustees must, first and foremost, act honestly in their capacity as trustees in all their dealings with the trust property. They must protect the property and only deal with it for the benefit of the beneficiaries named in the trust.

Identify the Trust Property

You must clearly identify the property to be included in the trust. If there is any doubt as to the exact identity of the property forming the trust, then the trust may fail for uncertainty.

Identify the Beneficiaries

Failure to correctly identify the beneficiaries will mean that the trust may fail for uncertainty.

There are three types of trust and each covers a slightly different situation but the information you have read above, is applicable to all trusts no matter how they are created. They are all dealt with as if they are created by will as this is the most popular.

1. Bare Trust

In a bare trust, a testatrix leaves her property to her trustees to hold the property for the benefit of her named beneficiaries until they reach 18. The problem with this type of trust is that the beneficiaries can access the property or assets as soon as they turn 18 and let's face it, most people are not really mature enough at that age to handle assets, no matter how substantial or insubstantial the assets are.

If you think your beneficiaries should have all of the estate at 18, then this trust is for you. It is not however suitable where there is a child or adult suffering from a permanent mental or physical disability as they will obviously require ongoing care. The mere fact of reaching 18 is irrelevant.

2. Discretionary Trust

In a discretionary trust, the testatrix will leave her property to her trustees to hold the property for the benefit of her children, but in this case the children may not necessarily get the property at 18. The trustees can, at their discretion decide when the children are mature

enough to receive the trust property. You should consider carefully who you want your trustees to be as they are getting very important powers under your will.

It may be wise to appoint a family member (someone subjective) and a professional person such as a solicitor or accountant (someone objective) as your trustees. Obviously, as parents know their children best, they can and should, guide their trustees as to what age their children might be mature enough to receive (and not squander) the inheritance. Whatever age they may be, the trustees can end the trust and give the property over and the beneficiaries are then free to do with the property as they please. But remember, you are leaving the final decision on this to your trustees.

With careful planning, a discretionary trust is very useful both from a legal and tax perspective. This type of trust is much more appropriate to the situation where there is a child or adult suffering from a permanent mental or physical disability.

3. Fixed Trust
In a fixed trust, the testator will leave his property to his trustees to hold the property for the benefit of his children. In this example it is the parent that decides what age the children will be mature enough to receive the property and the trustees are not given any discretion. It can be 18, 21, 23 or 25 or whatever age you think yourself to be most appropriate. Some parents think 'what the hell, let them have it at 21 and do as they please' which means that it is they who decide when the children get the property and not the trustees. You still have to appoint trustees to hold it until the child reaches the appointed age.

Other types of Trust
A person can also be a trustee for the purpose of signing a contract or legal document on behalf of another person provided they have been given power to act as such. Most trusts nowadays are created by will and they are created every day of the week in solicitor's offices around the country. A large percentage of trusts are for minor children.

A trust can also be created accidentally and while that may sound odd, it happens quite frequently. An example would be where you leave a house to a person for their lifetime (a life estate) but you do not appoint trustees. Here the trust is created by the very fact of you having created a 'life estate' without being clear as to what is to happen to the house when that person dies.

Breach of Trust

If your trustees are in breach of their duties as trustees, they can be removed. They either remove themselves by resigning their trusteeship or they can be removed where an interested person, usually a family member, makes an application to court to have them removed.

When does it start and when does it end?

A trust can come into effect on the happening of a specified event. If can be the date that property is put into the trust or more often than not, it will come into effect on someone's death, under a trust created by their will.

Trusts are ended or terminated on the happening of a specified event. Sometimes this event will be the death of a life tenant, when the property will pass to the person entitled to the remaining trust property or, the handing over, or vesting, of the trust property to the beneficiaries.

In some cases the trust property may have been applied for the benefit of the child's education and as such there may be nothing left in the trust when the child reaches the appointed age. In these cases, the trustees don't wait until the child reaches the appointed age but instead they will terminate the trust when all the trust property is gone. If the beneficiary dies then the trust can also be brought to an end.

Benefits and Pensions

In Ireland, Child Benefit (previously known as Children's Allowance) is payable to the parents or guardians of children under 16 years of age, or under 19 years of age if the child is in full-time education, FÁS, Youthreach Training or has a disability. Child Benefit is paid in the form of a monthly payment from the HSE. Child Benefit is not affected if a child receives a gift or inheritance.

Over the age of 16 (or 19 as the case may be) and up to 66 a person suffering from a mental disability may be entitled to a Disability Allowance from the Department of Social and Family Affairs. This allowance is means tested and any benefit received by way of a gift or inheritance may affect the amount of the allowance received. Many people believe that the State will provide for their children when they are gone. They may be mistaken. For full details you can look at www.welfare.ie or alternatively information is available from Citizens Information at www.citizensinformation.ie.

Duties and Powers *of your LPRs*

The terms LPR (Legal Personal Representative) or 'per rep' are used to describe either executors appointed in a will or the administrators where there is no will.

Consider carefully who to appoint as your executors. The job of LPRs or executors is time consuming and costly and although your solicitors do most if not all of the work, the executors carry the responsibility.

When making your will, you may appoint as many executors as you wish but as a rule, unless the Probate Officer otherwise directs, a Grant of Probate will not be given to more than three people. Two are enough. If one executor dies, leaves the jurisdiction or is simply unwilling to act, there is still a second to do the job.

You appoint executors in your will.

Who can be an Executor?

Your executor should be someone you trust. To avoid any procedural complications, appoint someone who is over 18.

It is a great advantage to have an executor who is younger than you and who has a good business brain. This is not essential as executors can hire accountants, solicitors and other qualified advisers to assist them.

You can appoint a beneficiary to be an executor. For a husband and wife where both are making wills, it is usual though not always the case, for each to appoint the other as sole executor and beneficiary.

A trust corporation can also be an executor provided they meet the requirements of the Succession Act. A charitable body can be an executor, although you must ensure that the charitable body is also a trust corporation. An accountant or solicitor can be an executor.

An executor can also be appointed by implication. This is known as an 'Executor according to Tenor'.

For example, John died. He made a 'home-made' will which stated as follows:

'My best friend Charlie is to look after all my debts at the bank when he is clearing his own debts. He is to clear all debts from the money coming in from the sale of land, and do all the paperwork with the solicitor so that my wife Zoe gets everything'

Even though Charlie is not formally named as an executor in the will he can be deemed to be the executor because he has been given the power to pay debts.

Bequests for Executors

It is a good practice to leave a bequest to your executors under your will. In the case of a family member it may be something large such as a house or some land. For a friend it might be smaller.

Bear in mind that your executors may be in charge of your estate for months or even years after your death until your estate is administered fully.

Names and Addresses

Ensure that you avoid confusion in the names or addresses of your executors. The same applies to your listing of beneficiaries. Family names are often handed down from generation to generation. Middle names or the term 'junior' or 'senior' can be used to help identify the executors and also beneficiaries.

Who cannot be an Executor?
Minors (Under 18)
It is not wise to appoint a person under 18 years of age to be your executor. There are two reasons for this. First, someone under the age of 18 is unlikely to be able to take care of your affairs after your death. Second, under 18s or minors are not permitted by law to take out the Grant of Probate.

Where an infant or minor has been appointed sole executor of a will, a Grant of Administration with the will annexed can be granted to that infant's guardian or any such other person appointed by the court.

Mental Incapacity
A person who is suffering from a mental disability of any kind should not be appointed an executor. If an executor becomes mentally incapable some time after appointment as an executor, a second executor who is mentally capable can take out the administration to the estate.

If an executor obtains a Grant of Probate and in the process of administering an estate becomes unfit to act, the court may revoke the Grant of Probate.

If an executor had made an Enduring Power of Attorney, it is possible that the attorney can be appointed to administer the estate.

Even if you do not have an Enduring Power of Attorney in place an incapable executor can be made a Ward of Court. The committee of the Ward of Court can then apply for the Grant of Probate to administer the estate.

The Probate Officer can, with the consent of the Registrar of the Wards of Court, issue a Grant of Probate to such person as they may deem fit.

Murder Prohibited
Interestingly, the law doesn't state that an executor who is guilty of the murder, manslaughter or attempted murder or manslaughter of the testator, is prohibited from acting as their executor. However, a beneficiary found guilty of such crimes is automatically precluded from receiving a bequest under the will of the person he had murdered.

If an interested person such as a family member, made an application to court, the court would remove 'the murderer' from the role of executor and would appoint someone else.

Do you Have to Act?
Someone named as an executor does not have to take on the job. An executor can simply renounce his or her rights under the will by completing a simple renunciation document.

Having signed a renunciation an executor cannot step back in to administer the estate in the future. The executor must not have 'intermeddled' in the estate in any way. If they have, they will not be allowed to renounce. It is a great honour to be appointed an executor. However, it is a responsible job and if you are not going to do the job, decide at the outset and inform the testator or the solicitor or beneficiaries of your decision.

After the testator dies, the executor will usually inform the solicitor. Of course, sometimes people don't know that they have been appointed executor so informing the testator will not be an option.

Executor's Duty

The executor's first duty is to lay the testator's remains to rest.

Believe it or not, the executor, not the family, has custody of the remains until burial or cremation. On the death of the testator, the executor should immediately look for and read the will. If the will had stated that the testator's remains be cremated, and instead the remains were in ignorance interred without cremation, the testator's wishes could not be said to have been carried out according to the terms of the will.

The instructions may or may not be part of the will. Solicitors keep notes accompanying the will in the testator's files. These notes may instruct on the form of disposal of the remains after death.

For Life

The duties of an executor are for life. So even if an estate is wrapped up today but an asset is discovered in a year's time in the deceased's (testator's) name, the executor has a duty to administer that asset in accordance with the will.

Administrators

An administrator is a form of legal personal representative or LPR appointed by the court and is usually the closest next of kin of the deceased.

The main difference between the work of an executor and administrator is that an executor can deal with the assets much faster, while an administrator must wait until he has what is called a Grant of Administration Intestate from the court.

An administrator cannot derive any power from a will as there simply isn't one to derive power from.

Died Intestate

A person who dies without having made a will or without having made a valid will is said to have died intestate. The estate is distributed according to statute or in other words the law.

The Succession Act not only states who gets what shares but also who the people next in line to act as administrators are.

The Succession Act sets out an order of entitlement to take out a grant for death occurring on or after 1 January 1967 and these include:

1. surviving spouse
2. next of kin as follows:
   (a) child or other descendant

   (b) father or mother, equally entitled

   (c) brother or sister

   (d) nephew or niece

   (e) grandparent

   (f) uncle or aunt

   (g) great-grandparent

   (h) first cousin great uncle or great aunt, grand nephew or grand niece

   (i) great great-grandparent

   (j) other next of kin depending on degrees of blood relationship with any direct lineal ancestors being postponed to other relatives in the same degree

There are other categories listed in the Act, the last of which is the State itself if no one else can be found.

POWERS OF LPRs

Power to Sell
The Legal Personal Representative has power to sell all or part of a deceased person's estate in order to realise the assets and pay debts, beneficiaries etc. The administrator can only sell from the date of the Grant of Administration.

Power to Act as Trustee
If you have a young family and wish to make provision for them in the event of your untimely death, you may name trustees in your will.

The trustees will hold your property in trust for the benefit of your children. The law gives the trustees certain 'powers' to do things but only for the benefit of your children.

Power to Appropriate - Section 55
The LPRs can appropriate all or any part of a deceased person's estate in order to satisfy the shares of beneficiaries in the estate.

Power to Appropriate the Family Home - Section 56
The LPRs can appropriate the family home in favour of a surviving spouse. The surviving spouse must be ordinarily resident in that house. The per reps must notify the spouse in writing of his or her right to appropriate and he/she must confirm in writing that they wish to appropriate.

Power to Lease - Section 60 / Power to Mortgage - Section 60.3
The LPR may from time to time raise money by way of mortgage or charge for the payment of expenses, debts and liabilities and any legal right of the surviving spouse. The LPR may also raise money with the approval of the beneficiaries or the Court for the erection, repair, improvement or completion of buildings or the improvement of lands forming part of the estate of the deceased. The LPR may also lease the property.

Power to Compromise - Section 60.8
LPRs have now been given power to settle claims and disputes concerning the estate of the deceased person without being liable for any loss occasioned by any act or thing so done by them in good faith.

The will also confers certain powers on an executor. These powers are sometimes required in addition to the powers that executors have under the Succession Act 1965. Such powers would include power to appropriate without serving any of the necessary notices or obtaining any of the required consents, power to invest or purchase unauthorised securities and power to employ agents/managers in respect of estate assets.

It is important to note that if the will does not provide these powers there is nothing which can be done after the deceased's death to rectify the situation, except a possible referral to court for directions.

Guidenote: Boundaries, One of the duties of an executor on taking charge of the estate of the deceased is to check the boundaries of the estate whether it is a house in a city or a large farm. Disputes over boundaries can delay the administration of the estate for months. To check the boundaries, a surveyor can compare the maps in Land Registry office or by getting copies of the maps.

Where the estate is a farm, check if utilities such as electricity and water are shared by adjoining farms. If this is the case, it will be necessary to check agreements. If the estate is to be sold, it will be necessary to cut off supplies from or to adjoining farms and to make arrangements for alternative supply.

Epitaphs

She always said her feet were killing her but nobody believed her.
- *Gravestone at Richmond,Virginia , USA*

Stranger, approach this grave with fitting gravity,
William Doyle dentist is filling his last cavity.
- *Inscription on the gravestone in Our Lady's Island, Wexford of a well known dentist.*

CARE

For most of us there will come a time when we will be less able to do what we did when we were younger. Less strength and less mobility are part of the life process. Less earning power go hand in hand with the process. You may have the opportunity to compensate.

Let us retain our dignity and independence. Let's make the most of the years when we should be taking it easy and smelling the roses by doing some care planning.

Making an
Enduring Power of
Attorney

The population of Ireland is growing older. Life expectancy at birth is 75.1 years for males and 80.3 years for females. According to the last census, which was in 2006, almost 468,000 of us are over 65. By 2030, that figure is forcast to rise to 818,000.

As the population ages, it will impact greatly on health and social services in Ireland. The elderly require four times the amount of health services of younger people. They are also far more likely to encounter mental health problems such as Alzheimers, Dementia and other forms of serious long term mental disorders.

At the time of writing, there are approximately 40,000 people in Ireland suffering from some form of serious long term mental illness. By 2026, estimates indicate it will be 70,000 and by 2036 it will be over 100,000.

If, in the future, you were to suffer from such an illness, it may result in you not being able to carry out the simple tasks of eating, dressing or going to the toilet without assistance. Quite apart, from the indignity to you it can also result in psychological and financial problems for your family.

You may need to be hospitalised or placed in a care home, or a member of your family may have to give up work to care for you on a full time basis, and there is of course a cost associated with that. Two costs in fact; the emotional cost and the financial cost. The emotional cost cannot be quantified and while insurance can cover the financial cost, many do not have it or cannot afford it, and so both costs are almost always borne by your family.

This chapter explains what an Enduring Power of Attorney is, how it can help you and your family and what happens if you do not have one. It should be considered as part of an overall care plan.

What is an Enduring Power of Attorney (EPA)?
An enduring power of attorney is a legal document that gives certain powers to whomever you appoint as your attorneys, to make decisions and act on your behalf in legal, financial and medical matters. The Enduring Power of Attorney Act was signed into law in 1996.

An EPA only becomes active if you become mentally incapacitated. The way in which you become incapacitated is irrelevant but it must result in you no longer being able to make informed decisions for yourself. It authorises your chosen attorneys to do anything that you would be capable of doing yourself, if you were capable.

How do I make One?
Just like a will, you might be able to do it yourself. You can download the Act from the Government website, www.irishstatutebook.ie, where you should find it among the acts for 1996, a copy can be obtained from government publications sales office on Molesworth Street, Dublin or you should be able to get it in any good book shop. Information is available on the internet too.

However, if you are serious about putting this document in place, visit your solicitor. Your solicitor will attend to everything, will draft the EPA, write to the attorneys, the notice parties and the doctor. He or she will complete all the necessary affidavits which have to be kept with the EPA in the event that it is ever required and he will store it for you.

What is Required?
In order to be able to make an EPA, you must be mentally capable of doing so. Your solicitor will usually be the first port of call and will run through a few issues with you to ensure that you are mentally capable. A medical certificate must also be obtained from your doctor.

To find out if you are capable, your doctor or solicitor may ask you to carry out any one of a number of simple tasks, for example, name the president of Ireland or the Taoiseach, count backwards from 100, add a shopping bill or any of a number of other tests. They must also be satisfied that you understand the nature of the document you are about to sign, the location and financial value of your assets and finally that you understand the powers that you will be giving to others in the event of your incapacity.

Chances are that if you have read and understood the above paragraphs you are mentally capable. However, it is a sad fact of life that outside of their own control many thousands of people who may be suffering from a dementia or a severe mental illness may be of unsound mind. If so, unfortunately they cannot make an EPA.

Your Attorneys
To make an EPA you must appoint an attorney though some people prefer to have two. Attorneys in this case are not like American TV lawyers. They are people such as your spouse, parent, sibling or friend, someone you trust to do things for you and perhaps take care of you should you become mentally incapable of doing so yourself.

In most cases the attorneys should be close family members unless you have genuine reasons for not appointing them. You can also appoint an alternate, or second choice, attorney. This attorney would only be required in the event that your first choice attorney did not want to act or is prohibited from acting or are themselves mentally incapable of acting.

Anyone under 18 cannot be an attorney. Nor can anyone convicted of fraud or dishonesty against the donor or his property. The owner of a nursing home in which the donor resides cannot be an attorney.

What powers will your attorneys have?
They only have whatever powers you give to them. This can be confined to personal care decisions, training and rehabilitation, housing, social welfare and so on. Or it can be a general power to act on your behalf in all matters.

The Law Reform Commission in 2006 has proposed amending the law on Powers of Attorney to allow qualified co-habitants to make personal care decisions.

You can make more than one EPA, appointing different attorneys to deal with different matters. You should choose your attorneys carefully as you are giving them important powers to act for you. If you give them general powers then they can sign legal documents, sell your house, access your bank accounts and other financial assets. They should be guided by your family, doctor and solicitor so that the right choice is always made on your behalf whether it is legal, financial or medical in nature.

Apart from the general law governing trustees, there are many fail safe mechanisms and protections built in to the Enduring Powers of Attorney Act. Your attorneys only get their powers when the EPA is registered in the High Court which means that you are no longer capable of managing your own affairs. They have no powers before that. They are trustees, meaning they cannot use your assets for their own personal use. If you have two attorneys then one cannot act without the other. If you direct that a certain person should be consulted about any particular matter then the attorneys cannot do anything regarding that matter without consulting that person.

Attorneys have no power to change your will, nor can they do anything outside the powers that you have given them. They must keep financial records of everything that they do in their capacity as your attorney and they must not mix their own money with yours. Keep it simple. Appoint people you trust to be your attorneys.

Notice Parties

You must name at least two people in the EPA document as 'Notice Parties'. These are people who must be notified in writing that you have put an EPA in place. This is to ensure that family members know what's going on. At the moment Notice Parties must be family members, in particular the spouse and children, but the Law Reform Commission has recommended that the law should be amended to include qualified co-habitants as mandatory Notice Parties.

If you later become mentally incapable then again they must be informed in writing of that fact before the EPA can be registered in the High Court. As they have the right to object to registration, this is one of the best protections available.

How does it work in practice?

If you have an EPA in place and are now becoming incapacitated your family will no doubt be the first to know. They will most likely contact your doctor first and this may be followed by a visit to your solicitor. Your solicitor will then see you and write to your doctor seeking a certificate stating that you are no longer capable of managing your own affairs. The solicitor must then write to your Notice Parties.

Once the EPA is registered, your attorneys then have the power to do all the things mentioned above. If you don't have an EPA then no-one can gain access to your accounts and assets. The emotional issues will be bad enough but to have financial worries now will just compound the problems, particularly if there is money there that could help pay for medical care. In these cases the money is simply 'frozen' and cannot be accessed without a Wards of Court office order.

Therefore the family must meet the costs of care and if the family is small then obviously the burden on each will be much higher.

Do you need an EPA?

You may not need an EPA. For example if you have no assets then it will be of little use to you unless of course you would like to give specific instructions regarding your personal care. If you have considered making or have recently made a will, then no doubt you accept the fact that at some stage you will die.

By putting an EPA in place you are accepting the fact that you might at some point become incapable of managing your own affairs through mental illness. If you have any sort of assets you should consider it.

If you don't have an EPA and your family need to have money released from your bank account and if the account is a joint account then the other account holder may be able to get access to money to help pay bills. Much will depend on the signing abilities of both account holders. Preferably both people must be able to withdraw funds without the signature of the other.

If you have no EPA, a member of your family can make an application to the High Court to have you made a Ward of Court. The family member, also called the 'petitioner', must swear an affidavit before a solicitor and the opinions of two doctors must be obtained to show that you are no longer capable of managing your affairs.

The President of the High Court must decide to conduct an inquiry and you will then have to be examined by a doctor appointed by the Court. If the Court directs that you shall be made a 'Ward of Court' then they appoint a person as your 'Committee'.

This will usually be the person who makes the Court application. Once appointed, you will come under the care of the 'Committee'. This does not mean that you must live with them as you may require full time hospital or nursing care. Your assets come under the control of the Court and money can be freed up if necessary. The law in this area is currently under review.

The Mental Capacity and Guardianship Bill was submitted in 2008 and it will be some time yet before it makes its way through the Oireachtas. If enacted, it will bring much needed reform to this area. It proposes to allow informal decision making for the care and treatment of incapacitated people and the appointment of a Guardianship Board that can in turn appoint legal guardians to take control of that person's assets.

The Bill can be viewed at: www.oireachtas.ie.

Difference between an EPA and a General Power of Attorney
A General Power of Attorney is different from an EPA. If for example, you were going to be out of the country for a while and you want to sell your house in Ireland, you can appoint an attorney to sign legal documents on your behalf to enable him or her to sell your house.

This is a general Power of Attorney. Unless you specify, it gives extremely wide powers to your attorney and they can do anything that you yourself could do. It is automatically revoked if you become of unsound mind.

An EPA is only activated when you become mentally unsound. Both die with you. You can of course create both as they cover completely different situations but they cannot operate at the same time. The confusion between the two kinds of power of attorney was the genesis of the Act.

Difference between an EPA and your Will
An EPA allows your attorneys to use your assets for your benefit while you are alive but incapacitated. Your will dictates what is to happen to your assets after your death. On death the executors appointed under your will take control of your assets and it is they who ensure that your assets pass to your beneficiaries.

Of course, if all of your assets have been used to pay for hospital or nursing care while you are incapacitated then there may not be anything left for your beneficiaries after you die.

Conclusion
If you have assets in your sole name, make an EPA. While you are able, you get to choose the good attorneys you want. Your doctor (GP), your attorneys and your notice parties all are made aware of your decision.

If you lose your capacity your attorneys can take care of you and your assets by freeing up money to pay any bills you may have, to get the care you require or the care you have specified in the document, to make your life as comfortable as necessary and to ease, at least financially, the pressures on your family as a result of you no longer being able to take care of yourself.

Providing Care Supports for Seniors

Nobody has defined when you become 'old'. We have met people of 100 years of age and they are as 'youthful' in their outlook as a 20 year old.

The age of 65 as the qualifying age for the old age pension was determined by a British civil servant 100 years ago in 1908. The age 65 has entered popular consciousness as old.

Today, 80 is the 50 of half a century ago as life spans have lengthened due to medical science, public awareness campaigns and knowledge about nutrition, physical exercise and managing stress.

However, even the Government has not really defined at what age you become old. Is it 45, 55, 65 or 75 years? They are similarly unsure about who is young. When are you no longer young? They have however, defined the cut-off point for young farmer entitlements to certain grant-aids at 35. Are you old therefore at 36?

We use the word 'senior' for those aged 50 or more as it bestows honour and acknowledges many years of experience. In talking about inheritance and succession senior is a more acceptable word than the vague word 'old'. You can refer to a younger person as junior.

Respect

If you are an energetic junior, you should recognise that seniors may have their limitations in energy. If you are a senior, recognise that the junior may be limited in wisdom and knowledge or may know more than you on many matters. That arrogant, energetic junior may be trying to help you.

Many people of 65 now out of the general workforce want to just sit and marvel about life, talk with family, friends and neighbours, watch the sun go down over the horizon and the dawn break next day. Or play golf!

Many feel that they now have freedoms and luxuries that they did not have before. They want to get out and make their contribution. They want to set up businesses, be advisers, and help their community.

Dependent

In considering the issues of inheritance and succession, it is inevitable that as you get closer to 100 your energies will become less and having been there and done that, you may care less too about greater achievements. You may be resigned to the idea of mortality. On the other hand this year a 92 year old Irishman completed an advanced computer course and planned to do more.

You may become dependent on someone else. You may have no one to care for you or too few to care about you. Your medical advisers have told you to take it easy. You are worried about your future. You have worried about others all your life. Now you are worried about yourself.

You don't want to put somebody else's life on hold. You are set in your ways. You want to preserve your dignity and independence. To change may be too much of a mountain to climb. You may get depressed and lonely very easily. Or you may be lucky and feel none of the foregoing feelings.

If you are a senior and have become dependent you may feel blame and guilt.
Blame - Why me? How could this happen to me? If only my family had... If only I had taken out an investment policy against my predicament? If only...
Guilt - My family do not deserve this. I am now causing trouble. I have to hand over all my personal functions, perhaps even some of my body functions, to a nurse or a doctor.

Be assured that unless you are very advantaged there are thousands like you. And there are and will be thousands in a worse situation.

But, be consoled too.

Host of Options

You have a host of options. Think of them in the context of making your inheritance and succession and investment plans. Here are some options to get you thinking:

1. Sell out. Leave Ireland and go to another country where property is cheaper and there are sun and beaches all year round.

2. Buy a property in the sun and spend the winter there and the summer here.

3. Go live in an independent living unit where there are like-minded others of your vintage.
   Advantages: In company of like-minded people
   Disadvantages: Confined, dependent on visits of family, friends and neighbours, you may get bored of too many of your own kind.

4. Go live with a member of your family if you have one.

5. Make an arrangement with a neighbour to care for you in your old age.

6. Book into a nursing home and spend the rest of your natural life here on earth there if you can afford it.

7. Get Private Home Care or get a Nurse to live in with you.

8. Go to a State-run geriatric hospital.

9. Stay where you are.

Of all of the above options, we encourage you to as far as possible focus first on the option of staying where you are if it's reasonable and if you have been happy there. If the 'system' works, be cautious about changing it.

The system could include a combination of family, community, neighbours dropping by for a five minute cuppa tea, doctor visiting, priest visiting, chiropodist visiting and home help visiting you.

Considerations

Whichever option you take may require a certain amount of planning and money.

You will have considerations of:
- Resources available to you - investment policies, land, house, savings, shares and so on.
- How to maximise your income by ensuring that you are receiving all of your statutory entitlements. For instance are you in receipt of the correct rate and type of social welfare pension or if you are not in receipt of a social welfare pension but paid PRSI contributions prior to 1953 are you entitled to a pre1953 Pro Rata pension? Have you applied for the Living Alone Allowance, Free Travel Pass, Free Electricity Allowance, Telephone Rental Allowance, TV licence and so on?
- Financial considerations and perhaps equity release from your home or property investment
- Family member who might take care of you
- Neighbours who might help you
- Medical advice where doctor advises that you need some time away from home to rest and be assured of medical and nursing care
- Whether or not you are eligible for a Nursing Home Subvention from the Health Service Executive i.e. to subsidise your nursing home costs
- Eligibility for hospital care
- Eligibility for home care
- Pension effects
- Tax and how it will affect you and your estate in your new circumstances.

At any age you will be able to figure out in general what your best options are. As a starting point contact your local Social Welfare Information Office, Community Welfare Office or Citizens Information Office and request a copy of the relevant booklets such as 'Checklist for Pensioners' and 'Entitlements for Over 60s'. If you have access to the internet at home check out the Citizens Information website at www.citizensinformation.ie or www.askaboutmoney.com website where with a little bit of work and patience you will be able to access much of the information you require. If you are a carer, or are being cared for, contact the Carer's Association, freephone 1800 240 724 for information about their services.

A System
Here's a system if you are living on your own:
- Home Help calls for two hours
- Neighbour A phones at 9.00 AM
- Neighbour B phones at 9.00 PM
- District Nurse calls every week
- You call to see doctor every month
- You take a car, wheelchair / Zimmer to the shops everyday. (Many 90 year olds are able to drive a car. If your doctor approves, drive away to your heart's content.)
- Priest / Vicar / Rabbi calls
- Family member or distant cousin calls
- Family draws up a rota to bring you out to lunch on a specified day each week

- You visit the local old folks centre.
- The Meals on Wheels people visit you or you may go to a local Meals on Wheels centre where you can have lunch and meet like-minded people for social contact and events.

If possible stay at your home. There are supports and services to support you in this option.

Avail of all available facilities. They are there for you. Wheelchairs, special bathing kit, railings, frames and so on are there for the asking from the HSE. Get in touch or get someone to get in touch with your Health Board for an assessment of your case. Enjoy your pension. Ask an accountant or good friend to check that you are getting your pension entitlements and bonuses.

Financial

Finance may be available to assist with payment for structural work in your home. For example you may need to build on, refurbish, take out your bath and put in a shower instead, widen doors to make it wheelchair accessible, repair the roof, have your house insulated and so on. Check with your Local Authority, Health Service Executive (HSE) Office or local Citizens Information Service to see if you are entitled to any of the many schemes and grants in operation such as Housing Grants for the Elderly, Essential Repairs Grant, Disabled Persons Grant, Rent Supplements, Heating Supplements, Exceptional Needs Payments, Home Care Grants, and so on.

The Warm Home Scheme

You may qualify (for a very small fee) to have your home insulated e.g. attic and wall cavity insulation, draught proofing of windows and doors, lagging jackets for hot water cylinders and so on. The only qualifying conditions are that you are over 65, own your own home and are in receipt of an old age pension and the free fuel scheme from Social Welfare. To find out who operates the scheme in your area, you may contact Sustainable Energy Ireland at 1850 376 666.

Security

If you live alone or with your spouse / partner and you worry about your security at home it may be worth investing in good security / alarm systems in your home. These can be purchased privately and vary in prices but for peace of mind it will be money well spent. If you can't afford to buy one privately there are also very good and affordable security / alarm systems which are grant aided by government and are administered through various organisations such as Neighbourhood Watch, St. Vincent De Paul and other such local organisations in your area. The Pendant Alarm System is available to seniors who decide to remain at home.

The 'pendant' itself is worn around the person's neck and if in difficulty you just need to press the button on the pendant and it will alert the Emergency Response Desk (053 937 6400) or Elderly Reassurance (01 413 0556) who will phone you straight away at any hour of the day or night and check to see what your needs are.

If you do not respond they will contact the various nominated people (three in total) and let them know that you have failed to respond to their phone call and that you may require assistance. If they fail to make contact with any of the three nominated persons, they will contact the local Garda Station who will carry out further checks on your home. There is a small annual maintenance fee for such a system but again for peace of mind it is money well spent. To find out the organisations that operate the scheme in your area contact your local Garda Station, Neighbourhood Watch or Citizens Information Centre.

Medical Card Entitlement

Check with your local HSE to see if you qualify for a Medical Card as this card is a gateway to a lot of services you may need if you decide to stay at home. As a holder of a medical card you will be eligible (free of charge) for a Public Health Nurse Service, Home Help Service, Home Care attendant service, wheelchairs and other such appliances you may need. The Medical Card will also ensure that you have free access to your chosen GP and free medication and drugs, dental and ophthalmic services and so on.

It should be noted that all those over 70 in Ireland are entitled to a medical card irrespective of how much income they have. For most people under 70 years of age a means test is applied. Remember that even if your income is above the National Medical Card Guidelines you may still qualify if you have special medical or social needs or if you have certain Social Security incomes from another EU state. As a first step apply for your medical card with your local

HSE office as it may ensure that the option of staying at home is more viable and long term.

Doctor's Options

Lots of elderly people fall down through no fault of their own. If you are elderly and have to be brought to hospital, doctors and geriatric specialists consider if you would be capable of going home following treatment? Or, if you would be capable of going home if support is provided for you.

Support could mean visits to your home of the Public Health Nurse who may assist with medication, medical dressings, and appliances. The Public Health Nurse is the person who can also assess your need for a Home Help who may assist with such things as shopping, lighting the fire, vacuum cleaning and so on or a Home Care Attendant who may assist with such things as helping you dress, toileting and bathing. As a general rule, either your GP or Public Health Nurse in your area is the first person to contact when you require such assistance at home. You can find out who the Public Health Nurse for your area is by phoning your local HSE office.

If your support needs are full time or you need help in addition to that given by the HSE you may need to seek assistance from organisations that provide trained personnel to come into your home and meet your needs e.g. The Carers Association or certain private companies that provide this service.

This can be expensive and there are certain limited financial supports to help you cope with the costs. For instance the HSE in your area may operate a Home Care Grant (Subvention) Scheme whereby you undergo a medical dependency and financial assessment and if you satisfy the criteria you may be entitled to a weekly grant towards your additional care costs. If you are caring for someone at home you may also be eligible for certain tax breaks so check with an accountant or local tax office for details.

If you are caring for someone at home you may be eligible for financial assistance from Social Welfare by way of Carers Allowance, Carers Benefit, Respite Grant and so on. If in this situation, you should contact the Social Welfare Information office, Citizens Information office or your local Carers Association office. The Carers Association provide a 'Carers Information Pack' free of charge which provides comprehensive information for carers.

Where staying home is not an Option

If the doctors and geriatric specialists think you are not capable of going home, you may have a number of options:
1. Private Nursing Home Care
2. Public Nursing Home Care
3. Sheltered / Independent Living accommodation where you will live independently but will have the necessary supports close by such as a Nurse, GP, Security system etc

1. Private Nursing Home Care

You may be able to reduce your nursing home costs by means of the HSE nursing home subvention. As a first step you should request and complete a Nursing Home Subvention application form available from your local HSE office. To be eligible for Nursing Home Subvention you must pass both a Medical Dependency Assessment and a Financial Assessment.

The Medical Dependency Assessment

This assessment is carried out by a designated assessor in your local HSE area. If you meet the medical dependency criteria you will then be assessed financially.

Financial Assessment

The financial assessment will be carried out by a designated officer within your HSE area. There are three main elements to the financial assessment:

1. All income is taken into account e.g. from pension or pensions, employment, letting of land, interest in a company or business and so on. Assessment of Means should be net of PRSI, Tax and Government levies. In the case of a married or cohabiting couple half the combined income of the couple is assessed.

However, the HSE should ensure that the person residing at home is not left with less than the current Non Contributory Old Age Pension rate as a weekly income. The HSE must disregard income equivalent to one fifth of the appropriate Non Contributory Old Age pension at the time. i.e. €42.40 for a person over 66 and €44.40 over 80 (2008 figures) This in theory means that this amount should be available to the person applying for subvention as a personal spending allowance.

2. Savings / Investments/ Shares / Money on hand deposited or invested etc. When calculating the income from savings / investments the first €11,000 per person is disregarded. There is no upper limit on the value of such savings / investments and so on. But a weekly income may be calculated from the combined values. In the case of a couple, the savings of the person going into the nursing home or monies held in joint accounts is assessable. The value of assets (savings, investments, home etc) may be assessed where the assets were transferred from the ownership of the person in the five years prior to the application.

3. Your home or principal residence. Income may be imputed in respect of your principal residence for a period of three years only from the date of admission to the nursing home. The notional income is calculated at 5% of the market value of the house and then divided by 52 weeks to give a weekly notional income. If however you decide to rent your home while in the nursing home the three year rule does not apply and the full rental income will be assessable for the duration of the tenancy.

No application will be refused solely on the grounds of the house value being too high. There are certain situations where the principal residence may not be assessed e.g. where the residence is occupied immediately prior to or at the time of application by a dependent relative i.e. spouse, son or daughter less than 21 years of age or in full time education, or a relative who is dependent on a Social Welfare payment or on an equivalent income regardless of source. There are other such examples where your home will not be assessed for instance if medical opinion indicates that nursing home accommodation will only be required for a short period i.e. not exceeding six months. You should check with your local Nursing Home Subvention Office for details.

When the medical dependency and financial assessments are completed, the HSE will notify you in writing of the amount of subvention you are entitled to if any. If you are eligible the payment is made directly to the Nursing Home and is payable from the date of application or the date of admission whichever is the later. In the case of an emergency admission, back payment will only be paid from the date of admission when approved as an emergency admission by the General Manager, Community Care services of the HSE.

You carry your subvention entitlement with you so if for instance you live in Wexford and you qualify for a nursing home subvention in Wexford but you wish to move to a nursing home in another county in Ireland e.g. to be near your son or daughter, the subvention is payable from the HSE in Wexford and you do not have to reapply from your new address.

The services covered by subvention include nursing care, incontinence wear, bedding, laundry services and aids and appliances necessary to assist a dependent person with activities of daily living.

If you are dissatisfied with the amount of subvention offered by the HSE you have a right to appeal the decision to an Independent Appeals Officer in your HSE region.

Nursing Home Subvention Rates

The rates of subvention payments vary depending on your income and assets. It should be noted that an Enhanced Subvention or a 'Top Up' subvention may also be payable in certain circumstances. In effect these are additional payments on top of your standard subvention entitlement, which may be approved by the HSE where the person's means and the level of subvention approved are insufficient to meet the cost of the nursing home care.

There is no automatic 'entitlement' to an enhanced payment and each case will be assessed based on individual circumstances taking into account the cost of care, availability of public beds and the means of the person applying and funds or assets that may be available to them.

You should check with your local HSE office for details of how this applies in your area.

The following charts provide some examples of how the basic nursing home subvention is calculated where a person has already satisfied the medical dependency criteria.

Example A

John, 82, is single and in receipt of a State Non Contributory Pension of €222.00 and has €11,000 in savings and does not own his own home. The Nursing Home Fees are €750 per week. His assessment is calculated as follows:

Income - State non contributory Pension	€222.00	
Income from Savings	€Nil	(as the first €11,000 of Capital is disregarded)
Income from Home	€Nil	(John does not own his own home)
Total Income	€222.00	
Less 1/5th NCOAP	€44.40	
Assessable Income	€177.60	
Income Greater than NCOAP over 80	€Nil	
Excess Means	€Nil	
Subvention Payable	€300.00	(Standard Rate Payable)
Plus Spending Allowance	€44.40	(For pocket money)
Total Subvention Payable	€344.40	
Nursing Home Fees	€750.00	
Less HSE Subvention	€344.40	
Balance to be paid by applicant	€405.60	

In this case John's nursing home fees are €750.00 and he will receive a subvention of €344.40 per week leaving him with a balance of €405.60 to be paid from his pension and his savings.

Example B

Paul, 82, is single and in receipt of a State Contributory Pension of €233.30 and also an Occupational Pension of €80.00 per week. He has €21,000 in savings and does not own his home. Nursing Home Fees are €750.00

State Contributory Old Age Pension	€233.30	
Occupational Pension	€80.00	
Income from Savings	€9.60	(€21,000 less 11,000 x 5% ÷52 wks)
Income from Home	€Nil	(Paul does not own his home)
Total Income	€322.90	
Less 1/5th State NCOAP	€44.40	(For pocket money)
Assessable Income	€278.50	
Income Greater that NCOAP over 80	€56.50	(€278.50 less €222 i.e. NCOAP)
Excess Means	€56.50	
Subvention Payable	€243.50	(Standard subvention of €300.00 less excess means of €56.50)
Plus Spending Allowance	€Nil	(assessable income greater than NCOAP)

Total Subvention Payable	€243.50
Nursing Home Fees	€750.00
Less HSE Subvention	€243.50
Balance to be paid by applicant	€506.50

In this case Paul's nursing home fees are €750.00 and he will receive a subvention of €243.50 per week leaving him with a balance of €506.50 to be paid from his pensions and his savings.

2. Long Stay Health Board Nursing Home Beds
If you qualify and take up an offer of a bed in a long stay HSE hospital a different method of assessment to the Nursing Home Assessment is applied in that you are assessed under the Health (Charges for Inpatient Services) Regulations 2005.

Under these charges your means are assessed but you cannot be charged more than €120.00 per week. Check with your local HSE office or with your Local HSE Long Stay Hospital to see how the scheme applies to you.

3. Sheltered / Independent Living Option
If you can no longer live at home but are still pretty independent, the option of moving into sheltered accommodation might just be the right option for you. You should contact your local HSE Office or Citizens Information Centre to establish the contact details of such facilities in your area.

Guidenote: Doctors often recommend that if you are recovering from a serious illness or a serious medical operation that you go to a nursing home for respite until you recover your strength. In many cases, they recommend that you go to respite to give family or carers who may have looked after you, time to go on a holiday.

Private Nurse
For a private nurse, it may cost between €50,000 and €100,000 per year.

However, this situation will not be practical in most cases. Apart from the cost, few nurses are available to do this work. The HSE provides home care grants. These grants may vary from one HSE area to another.

Perhaps, it may be possible for you to engage a 'mature' or 'retired' nurse to call occasionally to you on an attractive retainer paid for privately. If such a nurse were available, the cost could be considerable and there would be associated costs of tax, PRSI, hidden costs and so on.

Home Care Services
A number of home-care companies who specialise in nursing elderly and disabled people provide an excellent service for a fee.

Means Test

Your Health Board will carry out a Means test to assess if you are eligible for subvention. Your income and your assets will be assessed. You will be expected to submit your bank statements to the Health board.

Other Ways and Means

Assume you have a valuable estate. You may make an arrangement with a son or daughter to transfer part of the estate to him/her in lieu of your care for the rest of your natural life. However the Revenue Commissioners will be lying in wait for you and for your son or daughter. Your son or daughter may have to pay Gift tax of 20% above a certain threshold. You may have to pay Capital Gains Tax of 20%.

Another option for you if you are well off may be to sell a site to your son or daughter for say €60,000. This is less than the market value for the site. Assume your son or daughter can sell the site for €120,000. You will become liable to Capital Gains Tax of €12,000. It may affect your nursing home subvention.

If your son or daughter sell the site for €120,000 they will become liable to Capital Gains Tax i.e. €120,000 minus €60,000 @ 20% which is equal to €12,000.

There may also be a Stamp Duty liability of say €3,000. However they may have the sum of €100,000 to pay towards your nursing care. Of course you would have to take a leap of faith and they would have to make a commitment to you written down on paper in an agreement drawn up by your solicitor. Why not just sell it yourself and live off the money? There can be great difficulty and trauma in enforcing family agreements.

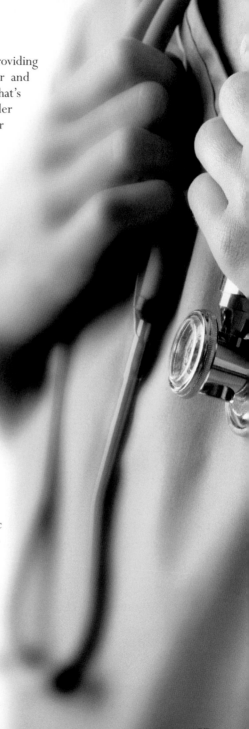

There may be other creative ways and means of providing for your nursing home care. A good solicitor and accountant/tax adviser will be able to tell you what's possible. If you have a business, consider transferring, leasing, handing over to a younger or more able person.

Our Advice
Apply for and get as many entitlements as possible.So many people do not take the opportunity. They lose out.

Before you Apply
Ask your HSE official or adviser to guide through the process before you make an application as you may become ineligible if you cross over the threshold by even one cent.

Residential Care
Only about 5% of all older people ever need residential or nursing home care. Residential Care is usually needed after a spell in hospital, where you are ready to leave the general hospital, but not quite well enough yet to manage at home alone. It can also be the best option when an older person becomes unable to live alone, through illness or disability.

There are two main groups of services - public hospitals and homes, and private nursing homes. -
From HSE website 14 April 2008

DEATH

Death comes to us all. Billions have died before us and billions will die after us. Let's not dwell on the moment of death. Instead, let's plan to leave this life as smoothly as possible when our time is up.

A good funeral plan will help to ease the decision making process during a difficult time for loved ones.

Handling Death &
Funerals

You may have a brass band or a marching band for your funeral. At the church you may choose to have flowers or no flowers. You may have a eulogy or no eulogy.

Few of us like to dwell on the process of death. But it can be made easier.

The debate about death is limitless. If you are an atheist, you believe there is no afterlife. Most religions inform us that there is an afterlife and that while our mortal remains may biodegrade, our souls or spirits will live on forever perhaps even through other lives.

Mortal remains
All that is left after your death are your mortal remains.

Because of the medication that is now available, it is statistically unlikely that you will die in pain.

Doctors, nurses, medical professionals and priests and vicars and rabbis know that people react to the news of death by going through a process of shock, anger, sadness, denial, depression, rejection, hope and acceptance.

At time of death, family, relatives, friends and the wider community in which they lived should be given space and be allowed to mourn. Sympathy my be expressed in different ways. It is often enough to just 'be there' for the bereaved.

Do you want your mortal remains to be interred in a grave or would you prefer to be cremated and your remains either kept or buried in an urn or scattered off a mountain or at sea to the four winds?

If you are a soldier your comrades may fire three volleys over your grave. They may end the ceremony by having a military bugler play the beautiful and haunting sound of 'Taps'. They may present the national flag to your family. If you are a Government minister, a whole array of arrangements and protocols will be put into effect.

Prepare in Advance
It will be of immense ease to your family if you prepare your funeral arrangements in advance. It will be part of a good legacy and good succession and inheritance plans if you at least leave some list of your wishes to avoid ambiguity or vast amounts of time and conflict in decision-making.

We all hope that we can die with dignity. Our funerals should be dignified and memorable.

List of Wishes
Do a list of your wishes *(See My Personal Affairs and Possessions List)* and give it to your solicitor and executors and perhaps a trusted friend. You can change it later if you wish. However, if you have one such list, it will help your family, funeral directors / undertakers and solicitor plan and avoid unseemly rows and conflicts over what they presume to be your wishes.

Your executors or LPRs are the only people who have authority to take charge of your mortal remains and your funeral arrangements on your death. From the moment of your death they take immediate charge and control of you and your estate. On your death it is their responsibility to make immediate contact with your solicitor to inform him or her of your death. Inform your LPRs or executors whether or not you have a donor card.

Guidenote: Take out a sheet of paper, and based on the My Personal Affairs and Possessions List, and the following list, quickly plan your funeral in about 10 minutes. Post it to your solicitor and undertaker. Then forget about it.

Here is a list of considerations for planning your ideal funeral.

Funeral Director / Undertaker
Appoint an undertaker and advise your solicitor and executors of the appointment.

Death Notice

Your LPRs may place a notice in newspapers and on radio of the time of arrival at church, the funeral service/ceremony and burial place and time. Your funeral director / undertaker advised by your executors should take care of the wording of the notices and placing them in the newspapers and on radio.

Contacts

Make sure there is a list of people that you would like to be notified of your death. They may be far away on the other side of the world. However they would like to know. And perhaps some of them are executors or beneficiaries.

Coffin

Decide on the quality of coffin or style of coffin that you wish to have. Ask your funeral director /undertaker for advice.

Funeral Route

The route that your funeral takes depends on many factors. It may be from a hospital mortuary to your home. It may be from the hospital to a funeral home and then to your home or to the church. Or it may be from your home to the church. The procedure usually is that your remains will be removed to a funeral home on one day and then to the church next day. Most burials take place within three days of death unless a post mortem has to be carried out.

In many areas there is a tradition that the funeral cortege will pass and stop briefly at the deceased's home or at a point on the road side close to it, en route to the church. Write what you wish to happen in this case but give some flexibility to your executors and undertakers to decide.

Funeral Ceremony

Decide who you would like to sing, play music at your funeral, and give a eulogy or an oration at your graveside.

Gifts

Select some simple gifts that are symbolic of your life e.g. your pen, a book, a golf ball.

Eulogy

If your church allows that a eulogy or tribute to you be spoken from the altar or at your graveside, tell your executor that it should be kept to no more than five minutes. Eulogies should be scripted and rehearsed.

Final Resting Place

There are usually restrictions by the local authority and by the church on where you can be buried. In many cases permission to purchase a plot for a grave lies with the local church sacristan or a church committee. Some families buy a number of adjacent plots to plan for their future.

Old Grave or New
Will your remains be placed in an existing grave which you would request the gravediggers to open or will you buy a new grave. If your remains are to placed in a family plot make sure you identify precisely the area within the plot where your grave should be and state it on your instructions for your funeral arrangements. At funeral time, many people become confused about the location of graves.

Gravediggers
Gravediggers in large cities may dig your grave as part of the service whereas in rural areas, the gravediggers may be neighbours or family.

Provision should be made to have gifts for the gravediggers. Provide refreshments for roughly two days of work – they often have to dig down through hard ground. Mini-diggers are used to open graves in rural areas too.

Laid Out
Laid out in suit/dress or shroud. Preparation of your body can include having your favourite lipstick /makeup on.

Book of Condolences
People queue up in their thousands to sign the books of condolences of dead kings and queens. So why not for you? Most funeral directors now leave a book or sheets at the entrance to the church or funeral home so that your old friends, neighbours and luminaries can express their fondness for you.

Such books are of course useful for those who wish to state that they attended your funeral, and would wish to have you send a memory card to them, keep on your relatives Christmas card list and so on. Many families love to keep the list or book of condolences as part of their memorabilia of you and your life.

Guard of Honour
Formation of a guard of honour is usually a voluntary effort by some inspired members of the community who wish to pay tribute to you and who are motivated to honour you.

Dress Code
Of the members of your immediate family, men may wear black tie and women may dress in black. Of course many regard black as outmoded and wear what they like. At some celebrity funerals, the mourners have worn white as a celebration of a life.

Wreaths or Bouquets

Wreaths or bouquets are discretionary. Should be left beside the coffin in the church or may be given to the funeral director / undertaker to put them in place.

Mass Cards or Sympathy Cards

To be left on the coffin.

Carrying the Coffin

Your coffin or casket may be carried on the shoulders of perhaps six chosen men of your family or preferred neighbours or friends or put on a trolley and wheeled to the graveside. If the chief mourners are elderly, or have bad backs and are unable to lift your coffin, it is best to instruct the funeral director / undertaker to have your remains wheeled to the graveside.

Walking behind your Coffin

In many areas there is a tradition of all neighbours and friends walking behind the coffin to the final resting place. If this is in a town or along a busy road your executor or undertaker should notify the Gardai if this is about to take place.

Lowering the Coffin

In your instructions, list who you wish to lower your coffin or urn into the grave. Between four and six strong family members are usually required to lower a coffin into a grave.

Music and Song

Your family and executors should in conjunction with the priest or vicar or church official check that rehearsals take place and that sound equipment, microphones and public address systems are in working order on the evening before your remains arrive at the church. Your executors and family can help decide who the singers and musicians are to be and what pieces of music and song to perform. On your funeral list, list the pieces of music and song that you like.

Priest / Minister / Rabbi...

Your spiritual adviser will be of immense help in the organisation of your funeral. They will have seen it all before. They will have seen grief at its most terrible and joy at its most heavenly. They will also be able to give your loved ones who are still on earth consolation in their grief and guidance during the grieving process.

Transport

Who is to bring the funeral party to your funeral? How many approximately will be in the funeral party? Do you want to include a long black funeral car to carry your mourning family? It can make a lot of sense to have a car that organizes the funeral party to arrive together.

Altar Servers

Ask the funeral director for guidance.

Obituary

Most local newspapers have an obituaries page. Obituaries are an important part of the social history of your area.

Afters

Refreshments / Entertainment for the funeral party / community - in a local hall (where the fare may be provided by a catering company) or a hotel.

Memory Cards

The publishers of Memory Cards will have scanned your name in t¹ newspapers and it likely that samples will be sent to your home address. You may decide in advance what photograph and words to go on your Memory Cards and have your executors get them printed and distributed to your list of friends, neighbours and those on the book of condolences.

Tombstone / Gravestone / Headstone

Your county council or local authority decides whether you can have a headstone and kerbing at your grave. Did you know that you are not allowed or should not erect a tombstone for about six months after the grave has been opened to allow the grave to 'settle'?

Headstone Inscription

Keep it simple. If you want an epitaph, make sure it is meaningful and not mawkish and cringe inducing. Best advice is keep it simple and to the point. Here is an example: Patrick Murphy, Gortnamuck, died aged 76 on 30 April 2010. Get a second and third opinion on the wording. Talk to a priest / vicar / teacher. Give a copy of it to other members of the family to check it for accuracy but put a time limit on their replies.

Mourning

Fifty years ago, you could not be seen to leave your home to go to a place of entertainment for at least six months after the death of your loved one. Today, there is no such obligation and most people get back to work and carry on. However, close family and friends will feel the loss and may be grieving for years afterwards.

Finances

The funding of your funeral is taken from your estate. Usually your funeral director /

undertaker will pay the bills including the offerings to the priest and altar servers and then reimburse his funds when your estate has been distributed in the months or year afterwards. Check availability of bereavement grant and also credit union cover to defray funeral costs. By taking an hour or so to imagine and plan your big send off, you can achieve the farewell and celebration of a life well lived that you dream of. Leave the living with fond memories of you and a knowledge that you have left no legacy of an unseemly family row.

Where you Die

If you die in hospital, you will be attended by doctors and nursing staff. If you die suddenly, whether it is in a road traffic accident or at home a doctor who together with the Gardai and perhaps a coroner will order your remains will be brought first to a hospital where a post mortem can be carried out by a pathologist and the cause of your death ascertained and certified. The Gardai usually await instruction by the coroner to transfer your remains to either a morgue or a mortuary in a hospital.

The cause of your death will be written on your death certificate which is deposited with the Health Service Executive (HSE) and becomes available to your next of kin or any member of the public through General Register Office Births, Deaths and (Roman Catholic) Marriages office, Dublin, or at a centre near you for example your local HSE centre.

Death Certificate

Immediately after death, the executor should go to the local HSE or Health Centre to ensure that the death is registered giving details of name of deceased, date of death, age, sex, doctor who certified death and so on.

The executor should ask for a number of copies of the death certificate as they will be required by the solicitors to administer the estate, apply for Grant of Probate, and release funds from financial institutions and so on.

If you die naturally at home, you have a choice of a wake at your home or in a funeral home. If you die overseas, and wish to have your remains brought back to Ireland, it may take some days to do so. Transport by ship or by air. Best leave such a complicated matter in the hands of a good funeral director/undertaker and your solicitor and executor.

Terms you may Need to Know

Embalming: cleaning out of body fluids and injection of a chemical to make you look as natural as possible.

Post-mortem: examination of your body after death to determine the cause of your death.

Death Certificate: issued by a doctor and placed on the public record and available for a fee from your local HSE Health Centre.

Inquest: carried out by coroner in a coroner's court to determine the cause of your death. The coroner's court could be in a town near you. Note that a coroner's court determines only the cause of death and not who might have caused it.

People's Preferences
Most people prefer to die at home.
30,000 people die each year in Ireland
More than 6 out of 10 die in hospital
-From report of survey by Irish Hospice Foundation

Executor's Responsibilities
Your executors or LPRs have responsibility for knowing of your death and for carrying out your wishes. When making your will, you should first seek the permission of those you intend to be your executors of LPRs and request them to immediately upon your death inform your solicitor.

This allows your solicitor to examine your file and consult any special notes or instructions from you that must be carried out. In this way, you will avoid a legacy of misunderstanding or mistakes that could have repercussions for generations to come.

Example
Testator died. His family instructed the undertaker to have his remains interred in a grave. The solicitor learned of the death through a newspaper report and phoned the family. The deceased's instruction was that his remains be cremated before burial.

Information for those Recently Bereaved
'Bereavement - information for those recently bereaved' is a joint publication from the Department of Social and Family Affairs and Comhairle. This booklet is aimed at those who have been recently bereaved and provides information and advice on the practical and material matters that arise following a death. It contains information on what to do immediately after a death, possible social welfare entitlements, tax, financial and legal issues that may arise and where to go for further information and support.

Guidenote: Bereavement Grant, A Bereavement Grant of a once-off payment for deaths which occur on or after 6 December 2006. Contact your local Social Welfare office or see www.welfare.ie or phone Local 1890 500 000 or 01 7043000.

Two Options
I had two options – get busy dying or get busy living. I choose the latter.
- From eulogy, and obituary in the Sunday Independant, on death of Det. Garda John Roche, baritone, who lived for five years following diagnosis of leukemia.

AFTER DEATH

The size of your estate, whether you leave a husband, wife or partner , whether you are divorced or separated, whether you leave children, brothers, sisters, parents or dependents will be issues of concern when you reach the end of your life.

How to distribute your estate, carry out your funeral, and pay your debts and taxes will be a major task for your legal personal representatives or in other words your executors. The rights of spouses, partners, children and beneficiaries must be taken into account.

We all like to be well thought of. Why not make it easy for those of use who are still here to carry out your wishes as effortlessly as possible and clear up any outstanding matters relating to your estate.

Why not leave this place in a better way than in which you found it, by leaving a legacy of happiness and harmony?

Distributing *your Estate*

When you die you lose direct control over your house, your land, your car, your pet budgie, your favourite piece of jewellery, your stamp collection or whatever constitutes your estate.

If you have made a will, your legal personal representative or LPR, or executor now takes control to carry out your wishes.

If you have made no will, or in other words have died intestate, the law appoints an administrator, usually your closest next of kin, to administer your estate.

Time of Anxiety

For most people, your death will be a time of immense grief and loss and memories. What you might or might not have left to them in your will or whether you have died without making a will may not even occur to them.

For some, this will be a time of intense speculation. Foremost in their minds will be the extent of your estate, if you have any debts, how much and more importantly to whom you have bequeathed anything. It's an understandable human response. For family and extended family, this may also be a time of extreme anxiety.

Solicitors see anxiety and concern a mile away. They see it every day in their work. They understand it. They see it in the faces of warring siblings. In some cases, parents may have bequeathed their estate to a son or a daughter who is seen by other family members to be undeserving.

However, regardless of what your family or siblings or others might have expected from your estate, your executors are obliged to put your wishes as dictated in your will into effect. This is known as distributing your estate.

Notify Solicitor

On your death your LPRs or executors should immediately notify your solicitor of your death. They should if possible do this on the day of your death. Give them the instruction that immediately on the day of your death they are to notify your solicitor.

In practice, most solicitors monitor the death notices in the newspapers and on local radio and will alert your executors. Your solicitor has no duty to notify your executors. That duty lies with your executors. Your executors should next arrange a meeting with your solicitor at the earliest possible opportunity to discuss your estate. Unlike what you see in American television dramas, the executors are the only people to attend. It is unusual to have a formal family meeting for a reading of the will.

To avoid uncertainty, advise your executors of your most recent will and also your wishes for your remains.

Reads the Will

On hearing of your death, your solicitor will search for your will, and check if it is your last will and testament, then read your will and if you have left any specific instructions about your funeral or burial, will advise your executors on the day of your death. For example, if it was your express wish to be laid out in a football jersey it would be too late following your funeral to carry out that wish. It is best to leave such an instruction with your funeral director or undertaker.

Your solicitor will arrange a reading of your will with your executors about a week after your funeral and burial. Your executors will be expected to attend at the solicitor's office where the solicitor will then read out the will in detail, taking note of his/her own notes used in drawing up your will. The solicitor will advise your executors on how your estate should be distributed to the beneficiaries.

If no Will

If you have made no will, you are described in law as having died intestate. In this case, your estate will be distributed as dictated by the 1965 Succession Act. In other words, according to the Act, one of your relations will step in and take on the task of administration.

We encourage everybody without exception to appoint a solicitor, make a will and appoint executors. Regardless of what you may hear otherwise, it is the safest and most efficient way to administer your estate. Otherwise you will be leaving a legacy of uncertainty, trouble, anxiety and upset to your family and friends.

Of course, not everyone will want to be an executor knowing the time and cost involved in carrying out the honour and the duty fully. You may wish to make some sort of provision in your will to compensate your executors for the time and costs involved in carrying out your wishes.

Assets

Assuming you have appointed an executor and have made a will, the duty of your executor will be, with the help of your solicitor, to gather together all your assets.

On the date of your death, all of your assets are frozen as at the time of your death and are now in the charge of your executor. Your executor cannot give away any part of your estate even if it's a thimble until all the legal processes have been dealt with, grant of probate obtained and the estate distributed according to your last will and testament.

Your Assets may include

- Your home if any which will be valued by an estate agent / auctioneer / valuer according to the value on the market at the date of your death.
- Investments which may include a house abroad, investment policies and so on.
- Bank accounts
- Pensions
- Shares
- Art
- Furniture.

Debts of your estate will have to be paid. These could include outstanding bills such as paying a builder for renovation of your home. A burden or debt may be written on the deeds of your estate if the bill has been the subject of a court proceeding and has not been discharged. Check your deeds in the Land Registry office for your area or ask your solicitor to do it for you.

Executors are allowed to pay certain expenses / liabilities of the estate before the residue is distributed to the beneficiaries. These expenses / liabilities include:

- Funeral Services Costs
- Funeral Catering costs
- Newspaper funeral notices
- Costs incurred in securing your estate following your death. These may include the costs

of installing an alarm and the costs of payment of insurance to protect the estate.

The process of Probate and Administration of Estates

My grandfather died 50 years ago but his estate was never 'administered'. Solicitors everywhere in Ireland hear this problem every day.

Thousands of homes and farms throughout Ireland have not been administered. The effect has been family disputes over ownership, uncertainty about the future, difficulties about management of those estates, legal difficulties and often a tortuous process in raising mortgages and loans for renovation or development.

In so many cases, it can also require time and huge amounts of money in proving the existence of parents and grand parents and even great grandparents through a genealogical research requiring birth, baptismal, marriage and death certificates of each person in each generation. Not only that but the cost of administering estates where there are a number of generations of individuals involved, can prove quite expensive. Layers of problems, including in particular, title and tax problems, build up over the years.

The word 'administered' is used whether or not the grandfather made a will. It is often used interchangeably to describe the process of 'taking out' or obtaining probate or the process of 'taking out' or obtaining administration.

Probate is the word used to describe the process of administering an estate where the deceased made a will.

Administration is the word used to describe the process of administering an estate where the deceased did not make a will.

In a Probate case the process is carried out by the Executors named in the will. Executors' powers stem from the will.

In an Administration case the process is carried out by a person called the administrator, who is technically appointed by the Law. Administrators in these cases are the next of kin and they are determined by the degree of blood relationship and the order can be found in the Succession Act. The next of kin are usually also the people entitled to a share in the estate. The administrators' powers stem from the Grant of Administration.

There are many other types of grants that may be required in given situations, such as Grants to Attorneys, Grants limited as to duration or purpose, Grants to a Committee of a person of unsound mind, Special Grants for illegitimate or adopted children, Creditors Grants, Second Grants, Double Probate and so on. They are not dealt with in this guide due to space constraints.

The Executors or the Administrators, both of which are often referred to as the 'legal personal representatives', usually engage the services of a solicitor to carry out the process. If necessary, the solicitor in turn will liaise with the deceased's accountant to determine if there is any tax liability to the Revenue Commissioners by the estate or any of the beneficiaries.

Probate and Administration involve, in simple terms, four phases:

Phase 1 - Revenue Commissioners

Compile details and valuations of all assets of the deceased and make and return the Inland Revenue Affidavit (also called the schedule of assets) to the Revenue Commissioners to decide what tax if any is payable on the estate.

Phase 2 - Get the Grant

'Prove' the Will or 'Prove' the entitlement of the Administrator. This involves obtaining the Grant of Probate or the Grant of Administration from the probate division of the High Court. These are obtained by sending the appropriate papers to either the Probate Office in Dublin or the local District Probate Registry, who in turn give you the Grant. Only when the Grant issues can the assets be collected, as the Grant is proof that the personal representative has the power to act in the estate.

Phase 3 – Revenue Commissioners (again)

Pay any tax due and obtain the necessary clearance certificates from the Revenue Commissioners and the Department of Social and Family Affairs.

Phase 4 – Distribute the assets to the Beneficiaries i.e. the people entitled. These are the people either named in the will or the people entitled by law to the estate under the intestacy rules.

It is essential that the people overseeing the Probate or the Administration check that all taxes are paid by the beneficiaries as otherwise the Executor or Administrator will have a secondary liability for those taxes. Primary liability rests with the beneficiary but where tax is due the solicitor will inform the beneficiary and the amount required for the tax will be deducted from the beneficiaries share. This is then paid directly to the Revenue by the solicitor.

This distribution phase can involve the sale of assets and the distribution of cheques or the placing of certain assets into the name of the person entitled. This can be a house, land, shares and so on. Distribution cannot take place until all necessary tax and Social Welfare clearance certificates have been obtained.

Estates should be administered as quickly as possible after the death of the deceased. Even the most straight forward administration can take six months and some can go on much longer depending on the complexities involved. If an estate is being sued by say a child under Section 117 or beneficiaries are squabbling, then this will result in delay in administering the estate.

Can you DIY? Yes, you can get a Grant or Probate or Administration yourself. The Probate Office and the District Probate Registries located around the country can help you with the paperwork. Getting the Grant is only one step in the process. If you decide to DIY you should remember that you will have to DIY on the tax returns to the revenue, the clearance certificates, the transfer of land or shares and the distribution of the assets to the beneficiaries.

All estates should be administered. It will ease the burden and the cost for the next generation.

MINDSET

Good planning gives you better control over your future. It gives you direction on how to use your resources whether they are large or small.

An ideal outcome from this planning may be your good health, provision for your family now and for your later years and your peace of mind.

To achieve a plan that is suited to you, requires thinking and writing and talking. It requires a mindset of openness and honesty.

It also requires an understanding that other people may have a different opinion, stance or perspective from yours.

People are Differerent

People are different. This affects their approach to dealing with personal, family and financial affairs. So it's no wonder there is difficulty in decision-making about property, houses, lands, stocks, shares or investments in transferring from one generation to the next.

There can often be family agreement. But this can be disrupted by one person being out of sync with group thinking. The ideal is to minimise the conflict between emotion and reason.

The decision of a parent can be interpreted by a son or daughter as reward or punishment even though the parent's motivation was only to do the right thing. This is regrettable but sometimes unavoidable especially when decision-making can be so difficult at the best of times.

A piece of property may have a different value to some family members. A family heirloom may be more significant to one and a piece of property with a current high value may be more significant to another.

Most members of a family may agree but one may may feel aggrieved over a small matter. It is important to understand that each person is different but it is important to also respect that difference.

Decisions

Decisions about what to give to others and in particular family members and friends can be a battle between heart and head.

An uninformed approach or decision can result in tragedy. That is why discussion and decision about the issues in many families is best handled by non-family qualified and experienced professionals.

Professionals who have an understanding and an empathy and sympathy with family decisions and plans are now in practice in Ireland. Don't be afraid to ask about their experience.

The Battle

The larger the family, the less is the likelihood that there will be agreement. Varying temperament types, family values, upbringing, religion, culture, community or societal background can influence decisions.

Historically, tradition dictated that the father gave the house or the land to the eldest son or daughter. For other members of the family, their 'inheritance' was the funding of their education. The eldest son or daughter looked after the property, the business or the farm and cared for the parents in their old age.

Currently with the appreciation in the values of property and the change in historical values, many people have developed a quantitative approach to inheritance and succession planning.

The values of one set of parents is to pass on the house or business or farm which they have inherited from their parents and in turn which their grandparents have inherited from their parents, onto the next generation.

The values of another set of parents may be to shape the future differently by handing part of their estate to their family, and some to a charitable cause.

Follow the Money Trail

Today, many parents will follow the money trail. A succession strategy may be to build an empire with the purpose of local, community, county or country or indeed world domination.

They may say that 'the farm is in a great location, but you can't eat or make money from scenery'. To families influenced by traditional values, this will be regarded as soulless or mercenary.

Is property and land a means of living and growing and supporting others? Or is it a means of commercial business driven by macro- economic policies of governments and profit?

How do we feel when we consider that the land or business that we currently own or are in possession of will be in the custody of a mix of people from many other races, religions, traditions and cultures within our lifetime? Can assets be protected and preserved?

How do we feel when the reality is that there will never be enough money from an estate for everybody?

The consequences of poorly planned inheritance and succession or none at all can be far-reaching.

Survive

Research in the US has shown that only 33% of family-owned businesses survive the transfer of the business to the second generation. There is similar evidence in studies in Ireland.

In other words, almost 70% of family owned businesses will probably be non-existent in the next generation.

We believe that many fail because of the difference in values and expectations of family members. The values of a father or mother or son or daughter may not balance with the expectations or investment of another family member. Expectations may be eased by telling others what to expect and what not to expect.

We believe that most fail because of either poor communication or no communication at all.

Some things are best said. Some things are best written.

Some things are best neither said nor written.

- Anon

Communicating
Interpersonally

Talk is cheap. But its effects can be expensive.

Talk is communication. Experts in communication tell us that it involves a sender, a receiver and a message. It succeeds when there is continuous feedback between all the parties in the conversation.

Body language is a most powerful form of communication. To better understand doctors, solicitors, mediators and counsellors listen not only to what people say but how they say it. They read body language also. Such body language can often reveal much more than words.

Sender

A father or mother or brother or sister or uncle or aunt or in-law or cousin or even a neighbour or friend may influence a family member unnecessarily with their own agenda. This may result in conflict without any apparent reason. Equally, the contrary can be valid. The reaction to that persuasion or influence can vary from agreement to resistance.

The outcome of the interaction may be that everyone wins. Or it may be that one gains at the expense of another and influences an outcome of disaster.

There are many kinds of senders of messages. One person in a family may be dominant. Another may be talkative and wear their heart on their sleeve and what you see is what you get. Another may be shy. Another may be manipulative. Another may be a combination of some or all of these behaviours.

Receiver
Then there's the matter of the person who is on the receiving end of messages. This person is in communications language, the receiver. Like the sender of the message, the person may have another agenda, may be deceptive or manipulative, may not be compos mentis or may just be easily influenced or coerced against their own better judgement.

Message
Central to the communication between two people is the message. If you have ever seen the workings of Chinese Whispers, you'll understand how a message sent from one person to another person can become distorted and be received as meaning something entirely different from what the original message was or was intended to convey. It happens every day.

People are complex beings and what seems logical to one may be illogical or nonsensical to another.

Family discussions on the sensitive and emotive matters of inheritance, succession, partnership, trusts, management, tax and so on may be productive in many cases. In others, they are either non productive or destructive.

There may be any of a number of different value systems such as cultural values, traditional family values or sentiment or remembrance of past events, both pleasant and unpleasant, at play in the minds of the different members of the family and extended family.

Breakdown
The employment of a mediator can be beneficial where it is likely that there will be conflict or breakdown on important issues. A quality mediator will 'listen' for all of the nuances and the feelings of each individual member of the family and will try to ensure that everybody feels that they have been heard. This makes it more likely to reach full agreement and completion.

An estate is finite and even if everyone in a family is apportioned equal shares of the estate, it may not be the fairest outcome from either a point of view of common sense or of natural justice.

Considerations may be:
- the welfare of the owners of the estate (property, home, land) usually the parents in their later years.
- the future of children.
- provision for people who have special needs including parents, siblings or children.
- provision for aged uncles and aunts and or extended family.
- provision for adopted or fostered children.

Values of the owners of the estate will influence decisions about the future of the estate by thoughts including:
- preserving the estate for the next generation.
- using it to provide for other members of the family.
- giving part of it or all of it to a charitable purpose.
- using it to create a dynasty or build an empire and so on.
- using it as a resource to develop a business.
- following the money trail.

All of these issues will come into play in the interpersonal communication of members of a family or extended family when making decisions about the many people who will or will not gain from the estate in a succession plan that takes effect in this life or in an inheritance plan that takes effect when you die.

Breaking the
Worry Logjam

Worry paralyzes millions of people unnecessarily. They don't know what to do or how to go about solving a problem or handling an issue. They procrastinate. They put it off to tomorrow and beyond.

If you THINK a lot about inheritance and succession your best step is to TALK about it.

DECIDE 1. What you want done and 2, Who to contact. Find the number. Lift up the phone. Dial the number and use the powerful underused word ASK to meet a professional adviser, accountant, solicitor, tax adviser, investment adviser, counsellor, trusted friend for a meeting to talk about the issues.

You have only one step to go - ACT.

One Bite

For so many people talking and thinking and acting on inheritance and succession matters is daunting. It is like being asked to eat an elephant. You may think you cannot eat an elephant. There is a way. Divide the elephant into bite sized chunks. Just one bite at a time.

This book is about life, living and putting your mind at ease while helping you to solve problems. You need not be carrying heavy burdens. Break that worry logjam. Succession, inheritance, financial planning and death matters are just one part of living.

With good planning and some qualified professional help, you can make living much easier.

Your Doctor

If you are your own doctor, we believe you have a fool for a patient. That is why we earnestly advise you to listen to an outside opinion. Accuse us professionals of being self interested if you like. Procrastinate and you'll increase the problems. Inheritance and succession are complex matters involving people, property, tax , finances and the law. You cannot afford to make serious mistakes.

Now WRITE IT ON PAPER. To help in the thinking process, work it out on paper. Allow yourself lots of space in a notebook to write it and re-write it again if necessary.

Start at the top of the page and write a headline e.g. My Inheritance and Succession Plan and date it. Focus on working on your plan for say an hour each day for a week. Watch your thoughts build up.

Most humans can think of only two or three things at a time. But if you think it out on paper, you should be able to consider all aspects of inheritance and succession more fully.

Having done this, write out a list of questions about the issues that concern you.

Next MEET. Bring your refined thoughts and your questions which you had written down on paper to your professional adviser and you'll make the most of the time and get the best possible advice.

Let this book be your guide in conjunction with your professional advisers to preparing you for planning your inheritance and succession.

So now postpone your worries and focus on your concerns.

You have begun your plan.

Good Books and References.

Here is a list of some good books and references that may help you to further understand the complex issues related to planning for succession and inheritance.

Men are from Mars, Women are from Venus by John Gray.

Families and How to Survive Them by Robin Skynner and John Cleese.

The Investor's Handbook by Barry McCall.

Investment Advice for Life by Marc Cunningham.

Loot by Eddie Hobbs.

Finance Annual by John Lowe.

The Land Problem, A Guide to Land Leasing by Des Maguire.

Farm Family Partnerships, by Jim Cleary, Ed.

Tax Savings for Farmers by Joe Hickey.

TAB Guide by Jill Kerby.

Family Finance by Colm Rapple.

The Irish Pension Board various publications.

The Incorporated Law Society of Ireland Publications

Law Society Gazette

Wills, Probate & Estates, Law Society of Ireland, Nuala Casey & others.

Succession Law in Ireland by James Brady.

Probate Practice in a Nutshell, by Eamon Mongey, 3rd Edition.

Tax Magic, by Alan Moore.

Health Service Executive (HSE) publications

Succession Act 1965.

Bunreacht na hEireann (The Constitution of Ireland)

The Richest Man in Babylon by George Samuel Clason.

How to Stop Worrying and Start Living by Dale Carnegie.

Don't leave it to the Children by Alan Crosbie.

ACA Farmers Handbook 2008.

Revenue Commissioners website: www.revenue.ie

Taxation Summary by Joe Martyn and Paul Reck.

Finance Acts.

The Guardianship and Capacity Bill 2007.

Comhairle website www.citizensinformation.ie

Stephenson Solicitors seminars.

STEP Ireland seminars.

Irish Farmers Journal, Hugh Scanlan's column.

Leabharlanna Fhine Gall

Useful Contacts and
Helpful Organisations

1. FAMILY AND SUPPORT

Treoir
14 Gandon House
Custom House Square
IFSC
Dublin 1
LoCall: 1890 252 084
Phone: (01) 6700120
www.treoir.ie

The Family Support Agency
St. Stephens Green House
Earlsfort Terrace
Dublin 2
Phone: (01) 6114100
www.fsa.ie

The Carers Association
National Office
Bolger House
Patrick Street
Tullamore, Co. Offaly
Phone: (057) 9322920
www.carersireland.com

Barnardos
National Office
Christchurch Square
Dublin 8
Phone: 1850 222300
Phone: (01) 4530355
www.barnados.ie

Irish Autism Action
41 Newlands
Mullingar,
Co Westmeath
Phone: (044) 9331609
www.autismireland.ie

Down Syndrome Ireland
Citylink Business Park
Old Naas Road
FREEPOST
Dublin 12
Phone: 01 426 6500
Phone: 1890 374 374
www.downsyndrome.ie

Enable Ireland National Services
32F Rosemount Park Drive
Rosemount Business Park
Ballycoolin Road
Dublin 11
Phone: (01) 8727155
www.enableireland.ie

Anam Cara
Child Bereavement & Counselling
www.anamcara.ie

National Disability Authority
25 Clyde Road
Dublin 4
Phone: (01) 6080400
www.nda.ie

Inclusion Ireland
Unit C2 The Steelworks
Foley Street
Dublin 1
Phone: (01) 8559891
www.inclusionireland.ie

Rehab
Rehab Group,
Beach Road,
Sandymount,
Dublin 4.
Tel: 00 353 (0) 1 2057200
Fax: 00 353 (0) 1 2057211

2. ELDERLY

Age Action Ireland
30 Lower Camden Street
Dublin 2
Phone: (01) 4756989
www.ageaction.ie

Alone
1 Willie Bermingham Place
Kilmainham
Dublin 8
Phone: (01) 6791032
www.alone.ie

Senior Care
Phone: 087 7590022
www.seniorcare.ie

Friends of the Elderly
25 Bolton Street
Dublin 1
Phone: (01) 8731855
www.friendsoftheelderly.ie

Senior Help Line
National Office
Summerhill
Co Meath
Phone: 1850 440444
Phone: (046) 9557766
www.seniorhelpline.ie

Emergency Response
Ryeland Road
Bunclody
Enniscorthy
Co Wexford
Phone: (053) 9376400
www.emergencyresponse.ie

3. Mental Health

Alzheimer Society of Ireland
Alzheimer House
43 Northumberland Avenue
Dun Laoghaire, Co Dublin
Phone: (01) 2846616
Helpline: 1800 341341
www.alzheimer.ie

Aware
National Office
72 Lower Leeson Street
Dublin 2
Phone: (01) 6617211
www.aware.ie

Grow Mental Health Movement
Infoline: 1890 474474
www.grow.ie

Your Mental Health
www.yourmentalhealth.ie

Mental Health Ireland
6 Adelaide Street
Dun Laoghaire
Co Dublin
Phone: (01) 2841166
www.mentalhealthireland.ie

4. GOVERNMENT AGENCIES

Citizens Information
www.citizensinformation.ie

Revenue Commissioners
www.revenue.ie

Office of the Data Protection Commissioner
Canal House
Station Road
Portarlington
Co. Laois
Ireland.
LoCall 1890 25 22 31
www.dataprotection.ie

Health Service Executive
www.hse.ie

Social Welfare
www.welfare.ie

Teagasc
Head Office
Oak Park
Carlow
Phone: (059) 9170200
www.teagasc.ie

5. FINANCIAL

Irish Financial Services Regulatory Authority
P.O. Box 9138
College Green
Dublin 2.
Phone: (01) 4104000
www.ifsra.ie
www.itsyourmoney.ie

Pensions Board
Verschoyle House
28/30 Lower Mount Street
Dublin 2
Phone: (01) 613 1900
Locall: 1890 65-65-65
www.pensionsboard.ie

Financial Services Ombudsman
3rd Floor, Lincoln House
Lincoln Place
Dublin 2
LoCall: 1890 88 20 90
Phone: (01) 6620899
www.financialombudsman.ie

Money Advice and Budgeting Service
Helpline: 1890 283438
www.mabs.ie

6. LEGAL

The Law Society of Ireland
Blackhall Place
Dublin 7
Phone: (01) 6724800
www.lawsociety.ie

Property Registration Authority
Chancery Street
Dublin 7
Phone: (01) 6707500
www.landregistry.ie

Courts Service
15/24 Phoenix Street North
Smithfield
Dublin 7
Phone: (01) 8886000
www.courts.ie

Legal Aid Board
Head Office
Quay Street
Cahirciveen
Co Kerry
Phone: (066) 9471000
LoCall: 1890 615200
www.legalaidboard.ie

Free Legal Advice Centres
Head Office
13 Lower Dorset Street
Dublin 1
Phone: (01) 8745690
www.flac.ie

you matter...